AF380146

La Biennale di Venezia

60. Esposizione Internazionale d'Arte

Partecipazioni Nazionali

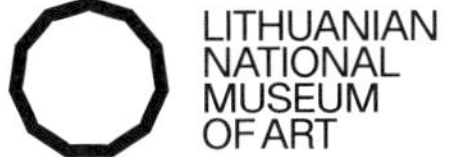

Mousse Publishing

Vilnius-Milan   2024

Organizer: 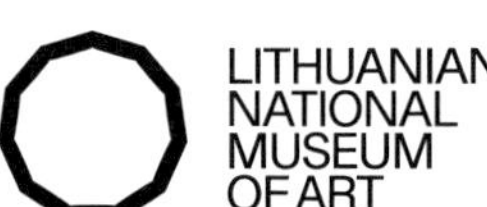 LITHUANIAN NATIONAL MUSEUM OF ART

Commissioned by: 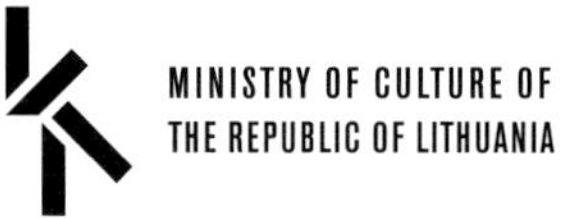 MINISTRY OF CULTURE OF THE REPUBLIC OF LITHUANIA

Financed by: 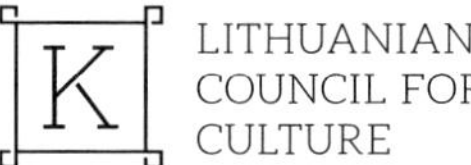 LITHUANIAN COUNCIL FOR CULTURE

Partners: carlier | gebauer 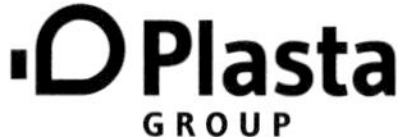 Plasta GROUP

Sponsors: 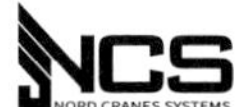 NORD CRANES SYSTEMS 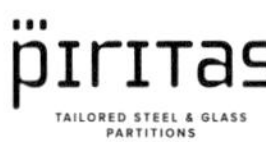 piritas TAILORED STEEL & GLASS PARTITIONS 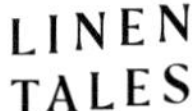 LINEN TALES NOEWE FOUNDATION EXTERUS dedicated to walls GLASSIC

Media sponsors: 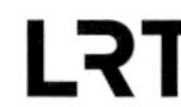 LRT JCDecaux art news.lt

EXHIBITION

Republic of Lithuania
60th International Art Exhibition
La Biennale di Venezia
Chiesa di Sant'Antonin
19 April–31 October 2024

Pakui Hardware and Marija Teresė Rožanskaitė
INFLAMMATION

Producer of the exhibition: The Lithuanian National Museum of Art

Artists: Pakui Hardware (Neringa Černiauskaitė, Ugnius Gelguda) and Marija Teresė Rožanskaitė
Curators of the pavilion: Valentinas Klimašauskas, João Laia
Commissioner of the pavilion: Arūnas Gelūnas
Exhibition environment and landscape architects: Išora x Lozuraitytė Studio
Light artist: Eugenijus Sabaliauskas
Design: Vytautas Volbekas
Coordinators: Evaldas Stankevičius, Egla Mikalajūnė
Architect coordinator: Eglė Jagminė
Public relations' producer: Rūta Statulevičiūtė-Kaučikienė

Special thanks: Algė Andriulytė, Micola Clara Brambilla, Laura Gabrielaitytė-Kazulėnienė, Lolita Jablonskienė, Aušrinė Mačėnienė, Jolanta Marcišauskytė-Jurašienė, Gediminas Mikelaitis, Mindaugas Reklaitis, Arūnas Steponėnas, Marco Scurati

TABLE OF CONTENTS

Arūnas Gelūnas

**Commissioner of the Lithuanian Pavilion
at the 60th Edition of La Biennale di Venezia**

The Inflammation of Saint Anthony: Commissioners' Word

Why would anyone want to read an introductory text by the commissioner of the national pavilion and not just jump ahead (I believe many will have already done this, and so will never read this in any way) to the texts by the curators and artists themselves? I could think of at least one reason: the commissioner sees all the beauty and complexity of the interplay of imagination and passion among the artists, the intelligence and insight of the curators, and the vision and ingenuity of the architects, and thus might provide a bit of a bird's-eye view of these orchestral maneuvers in the pavilion space that he or she is responsible of providing with "all-inclusive" services.

The Lithuanian national pavilion at La Biennale di Venezia this year showcases a unique constellation of three duos: Pakui Hardware, the artistic duo of Neringa Černiauskaitė and Ugnius Gelguda; the curatorial duo of Valentinas Klimašauskas and João Laia; and the duo of architects Ona Lozuraitytė and Petras Išora. Finally, the artwork itself, *Inflammation*, also has a somewhat dual nature, given the coexistence of Pakui Hardware's contemporary installation and the modern figurative paintings by the late Marija Teresė Rožanskaitė. All the duos are internationally renowned creators highly regarded in their respective professional circles. And what emerges from this collaboration is indeed a synergetic flow of intertwining individual voices—a mesmerizing, dreamlike art-work the authors like to call "a state of mind." It is also Lithuania's thirteenth time at La Biennale di Venezia, which may inspire the superstitious among you to shiver a bit!

Today, as I write this, we have already walked the walk that looks like quite a long journey. One of the reasons is "the challenge of the venue." In contrast to the countries that have pavilion spaces guaranteed for each edition of the Biennale, Lithuania has only freed itself from Soviet occupation since 1990 and thus has to look for a new pavilion space for every edition (and since 1999 there have only been two cases when the same venue was used a second time). Often this provides new stimulus for artistic and/or architectural solutions, and this year, that has been exactly the case.

After engaging in the usual research odyssey, as we called it, we all decided that the magnificent historical interior of the Chiesa di Sant'Antonin was exactly the space for *Inflammation*. Coming from the city of Vilnius, known for its thirty-seven Baroque churches, we felt it quite natural (or was it a subconscious drive?) to transplant the Pakui Hardware installation from the Arsenal of Arms, built in the 1560s and today home to the Museum of Applied Arts and Design, a branch of the Lithuanian National Museum of Art, where it had its first "rehearsal" in front of a Lithuanian audience, to the church space in Venice. A church named for Saint Anthony.

Even though the semantic links between Pakui Hardware's installation and the biblical narrative of the Temptations of Saint Anthony are not so direct, one detail seems obviously similar: the desert. Anthony perceived his sainthood and met his demons in the desert, and this is also where Pakui Hardware's creatures live—the desert of plastic residue. Artists would hate for us to think about their works as straightforwardly apocalyptic, but the first association that arises, in my mind at least, is that of global pollution and climate change. These circumstances alone would be enough to consider the topic of *Inflammation* if we had not also had two years of COVID-19 and two years of war in Ukraine (very close to Lithuanian borders). And then Gaza. There are, needless to say, many more contexts for *Inflammation*, but I cannot avoid saying here that I consider

Pakui Hardware's work almost prophetic. The aspect that, again, seems to fit the space of Sant'Antonin very well.

There is also an institutional circumstance. I am very proud and thankful that the cooperation between Pakui Hardware and the Lithuanian National Museum of Art has resulted in the production of their artwork at La Biennale di Venezia. This has led to a whole series of inspiring partnerships, for instance with the gallery carlier | gebauer, which has represented Pakui Hardware so successfully for the last ten years, and with the Plasta factory, which provided the plastic for the plastic desert. We must also thank our magnificent agent, Marco Scurati, who introduced us to Don Gianmatteo Caputo, head of the Chiesa di Sant'Antonin. I am very thankful to my colleagues Arūnas Steponėnas, Evaldas Stankevičius, Rūta Statulevičiūtė-Kaučikienė, Egla Mikalajūnė, Eglė Jagminė, and many others for being such a fantastic, dynamic team and invaluable companions in this "journey to a desert"—a journey whose end cannot yet be foreseen.

You, kind visitors and readers of this catalogue, are very welcome to join us here and experience *Inflammation* in the contemplative and thoughtful way the artists hope and expect that you will.

Valentinas Klimašauskas, João Laia

Curators of the Lithuanian Pavilion
at the 60th Edition of La Biennale di Venezia

Inflammation
Pakui Hardware and Marija Teresė Rožanskaitė

This project brings together the distinct experiences of artists belonging to two generations and explores the inflammation of (post)human bodies under today's economic and social conditions. Marija Teresė Rožanskaitė's paintings and a sculptural installation by Pakui Hardware (with assistance from the architectural duo Išora x Lozuraitytė) are connected by themes of medicine and hospitals, as well as natural, cosmic, and industrial landscapes. The combined presentation conveys the interconnectedness of bodies and environments in crisis while offering a metabolic balance, helping to "cool" the burning human and planetary bodies.

The fused aluminum and glass sculptures by Pakui Hardware resemble enlarged nervous systems and swollen organs. They were molded on scorched earth (the aluminum elements) and shaped in sweltering heat (the glass elements). Like bodies, they come to life when touched by a burning beam that resemble spatial or organ scanning. The prosthetic motif—using silicone membranes and medical or laboratory materials—is further expanded by the connections between the individual elements, which merge into a larger unified installation, a techno-organism.

In the paintings by Rožanskaitė, unnamed diseases, sterile operating theaters and medical consultation rooms, visceral-themed assemblages, and machine-like objects irradiate a chronic inflammation of the cosmic flesh. The works refer to abandoned, exploited carcasses—well-being ripped from human life.

The project draws direct inspiration from Marya Rupa and Raj Patel's 2021 book *Inflamed: Deep Medicine and the Anatomy of Injustice*, which invokes inflammation as a metaphor for the systemic harm being inflicted on humanity and the planet. Inflammation, according to the authors, is the body's normal response to toxic conditions, and the most urgent things to be "treated" are not individual unhealthy organs but the very systems—economic and social—that cause chronic ailments be passed from one generation to the next. The book and the exhibition connect the human and the planetary scales: not only are our bodies aflame, but so is the Earth. Another critical thread, which has also been evolving in the artists' work, is the questioning of Western cosmology, characterized by a constant fragmentation or separation—of mind from body, of human from nature, of what is considered "our own" from what belongs to the realm of "the other."

Accordingly, in this delirious post-landscape, it is difficult to distinguish between what is attributed to nature and what is considered a human creation. Objects referring to human bodily systems in a state of inflammation, architecture, a post-natural landscape of plastic soil, light, and other technologies merge into a unified hybrid techno-organism.

Valentinas Klimašauskas

**Curator of the Lithuanian Pavilion
at the 60th Edition of La Biennale di Venezia**

Chronic States: Cosmic Wounds, Inflamed Nervous Systems, and Hope (?) Station

As we explore inflammation in this book, we will sometimes use the language of the body in analogy. So: salmon are to rivers as hearts are to blood vessels. They both function as nutrient pumps in systems of circulation. We sometimes proceed by simile: dams are like vascular obstructions. We're not above metaphor. Trade routes, for example, are colonialism's arteries, moving people, capital, goods, and diseases around the world system, and connecting bodies, societies, geographies, and ecologies. The metaphor helps us to show that inflammation is systemic and that the systems are linked. But we aren't making a literary argument so much as a medical one. The inflammation in your arteries and the inflammation of the planet are linked, and the causal connections are becoming increasingly clear; your physiological state is a reaction to social and environmental factors. Racial violence, economic precarity, industrial pollution, poor diet, and even the water you drink can inflame you.

—Rupa Marya and Raj Patel, *Inflamed: Deep Medicine and the Anatomy of Injustice*, 2021[1]

CHRONIC STATES

Let's start with something persistently unenthusiastic. Let's start with a statement that the prolonged and long-overdue stage of conversion, shifting, and transition, mostly through systemic inflammation, burnout, and heat, is one of the burning themes, the smoldering conditions, of the current world and of this exhibition. The many ongoing conversions from various crises into a more fair present seem chronic and inactive. The shifting is dragging and bleeding. The transitioning is procrastinated and systematically delayed. Referring to the times of multiple crises, the exhibition radiates through various bodies, materials, and painterly narratives about prolonged inflammation on human and cosmic levels. "Your body is inflamed. If you haven't felt it yet, you or someone close to you soon will. Symptoms to look for include uncontrolled weight gain or unexpected weight loss, skin rashes, difficulty with memory, fever, trouble breathing, and chest pain." In medicine, the typical role of bodily inflammation is to remove the root cause of cell injury, eliminate necrotic cells and damaged tissues, and kick-start healing. Normally, inflammation is not a disease but a vital part of recuperation. But the current sociopolitical and other climates of the world are arranged to burn and char due to the systemic toxicity of how the world is (dis)organized.

"Your body is part of the society inflamed." I, one of the inflamed, write this text, first of all, thinking about the methodology as mentioned above in *Inflamed: Deep Medicine and the Anatomy of Injustice* (2021) by Rupa Marya and Raj Patel—using the language of the body in analogy, avoiding being "above metaphor," introducing artists' work while, at the last chapter, connecting them to pagan Lithuanian rites and landscapes. This kind of vision entangles long-stressed bodies, organs, nervous and other systems, heat, metaphors, and narratives. It also potentially allows us to understand and describe the current intertwined multiple crises better and likely could open up more interpretive meanings inscribed in the exhibition. And while wandering through it, questions may arise about what aesthetic

1   Unless otherwise mentioned, all quotes are excerpts from Rupa Marya and Raj Patel, *Inflamed: Deep Medicine and the Anatomy of Injustice* (New York: Farrar, Straus and Giroux, 2021), ebook.

sociopolitical conditions and resolutions, if any, unite the works by two different generations of Lithuanian artists, Pakui Hardware and Marija Teresė Rožanskaitė, under this specific aforementioned theme of inflammation. Let's take a few possible paths to answer the question.

MARIJA TERESĖ ROŽANSKAITĖ AND COSMIC WOUNDS

In the oeuvre of the modernist painter Marija Teresė Rožanskaitė (1933–2007), unnamed omnipresent disease, sterile operating rooms, hospitals, sore flesh-themed assemblages, paintings, and objects irradiate chronic inflammation of the cosmic flesh. Since she was an emerging artist, Rožanskaitė turned her attention to far-from-obvious themes in Lithuanian painting—she made a series of works about ecological, social, historical, and political concerns. To give more detailed examples, Rožanskaitė made exhibitions about female bodies in the Soviet medical system and about female conditions in general, Soviet deportations to Siberia (she was sent with her family to Siberia when she was eleven years old and returned with her mother when she was fourteen), and various care-related themes, for instance about Mother Teresa, nuns, Chechen women, et cetera. It is not difficult to notice that from space fantasy, cosmic composition, to heart surgery, an open heart (?), the subjects of Rožanskaitė's paintings share some complex biological and metaphysical response to the current state of affairs.

One of the most repetitive yet enigmatic painterly motifs in Rožanskaitė's paintings is the trope of the cut, the hole, or some kind of metaphysical portal, a (psycho) active cavity that could be taking a shape of a malformed heart, vagina (?), damaged cancerous or immune cells, or just a (semi) abstract opening. This perplexing cut could be understood as some kind of metaphor for ongoing global and bodily inflammation, continuing on micro and/or macro levels. In *Space Fantasy* (1979) or *Disease* (1985) we see a black hole in the shape of what may be named a heart; in *Reinforcement Rods* (1986) the cut opens up a belly; in *Cosmic*

Composition (1979) this phenomenon may be interpreted as black pathogens, damaged cells, irritants, a protective response that may or may not involve immune cells, blood vessels, and molecular mediators. In *Heart Surgery* (1974) it could be interpreted as some kind of levitating cosmic aorta or vulva. In *Heart* (1987) the blurred white gleams like an iridescent reflection of operating room lights or a still-shaping space portal. The enigmatic openings may be interpreted as open cosmic wounds, metaphysical portals, or hyperobjects, that last a term by philosopher Timothy Morton defined as an object that is interconnected, being massively distributed in time and space, making complex systems that challenge our traditional understanding of objects as discrete, localized entities. One may speculate if Rožanskaitė proposed to look at the aforementioned reappearing symbols of a cut, hole, vagina (?), or wound as if they were somehow interconnected in the texture or material of the universe, signaling or even connecting the wounds and "inflammations in your arteries and the inflammation of the planet," to quote again Marya and Patel.

PAKUI HARDWARE AND INFLAMED NERVOUS SYSTEM AND FLESH

The themes and keywords of interconnected human and exo bodies, organs, organisms, and their metabolisms and plasticity in various environments, from petri dishes and sterile operation rooms to speculative shamanist environments, have been reappearing since Pakui Hardware's first solo exhibition at the Contemporary Art Centre in Vilnius in 2014. To freely quote various texts on the exhibitions, in *The Return of Sweetness* (Tenderpixel, London, 2018),[2] they explored "metabolism both as a metaphorical device and as a physical and biological process." *Extrakorporal* (Bielefelder Kunstverein, Germany, 2018) immersed the viewer in a petri dish where "organs and tissues grow outside bodies, the future behavior of which is still a matter for speculation."[3] In *Underbelly* (MdBK Leipzig, 2019) viewers could enter an oversize belly with "transparent quasi-familiar objects" that "resemble enlarged organisms."[4] *Thrivers* (Polansky

2 https://echogonewrong.com/return-sweetness-pakui-hardware-tenderpixel-london/.
3 https://artviewer.org/pakui-hardware-at-bielefelder-kunstverein/.
4 https://www.moussemagazine.it/magazine/pakui-hardware-underbelly-at-mdbk-leipzig-2019-2020/.

Gallery, Prague, 2019) presented "a setting for unresolved figures that merge human limbs with diverse bodies of extremophiles. Thriving under harsh environmental conditions such as extreme cold, heat, acidity or radiation, extremophiles are massaging us for the upcoming future scenarios."[5] *Absent Touch* (carlier | gebauer, Berlin, 2020) focused "on the recent rise of remote-healthcare technologies and services, a phenomenon also known as 'virtual care,' that encompasses telemedicine, telehealth and robotic surgery."[6]

Although one may trace similarities between Pakui Hardware and Rožanskaitė in their interests in the wider interpretations of bodies, organs, flesh, hospital, and surgery spaces, it was at their solo exhibition *Virtual Care* (Baltic Centre for Contemporary Art, Gateshead, UK, 2021) when Pakui Hardware openly acknowledged in the exhibition text that Rožanskaitė's legacy inspired the treatment of the bodies:

> The space was transformed into an environment that resembles a clinical surgery room where human presence—with the exception of the visitor themselves—is replaced by technology. . . . Suspended between physical and virtual, bodily and digital, transparent thermoformed or resin "bodies" [were] abstracted into sculptural biomorphic shapes that [were] both present and erased at the same time. Partially inspired by paintings by Lithuanian artist Teresė Rožanskaitė from the 1970s and 80s, these "bodies" [were] traces, shells of "flesh," dominated by technology.[7]

The theme of drained bodies and inflamed organs that are being "scanned" or X-rayed by medicinal apparatuses is even more urgent and pressing in the current exhibition. In *Inflammation* (a 2023 solo exhibition at the Museum of Applied Arts and Design, Vilnius, and a two-person show in 2024 with Rožanskaitė at La Biennale di Venezia) we encounter sculptural figures that resemble prosthetic organs and silhouettes of drained nervous systems. Pakui Hardware uses carcasses, and formalized medicinal structures of support, the motif of prostheses—using silicone membranes, and medical or laboratory materials.[8] The aforementioned prostheses and sculptural carcasses of chronically inflamed nervous systems are interconnected into this techno-organism, possibly into some kind of station of care (?) and hope (?) in permanent transition.

Let's talk about it in the next chapter.

HOPE (?): INSTALLATION AS A TRANSITION STATION

Hope is as chronic as inflammation. How may we foresee it arising at this very dark hour of recent human history despite how naive that may sound?

One of the reasons to be hopeful is the fact of this untimely collaboration between artists of different generations. The inflammation does not belong to our generation only—Rožanskaitė proved it in her work many times. Think of the centuries of extraction and enslavement Marya and Patel also caution about in their book. Thematically and formally, the works by Pakui Hardware and Rožanskaitė overlap in the use of empty bodies and organs that look like traces and shells of flesh, exhausted carcasses, or exo bodies that are incorporated into what comes after nature but before culture sets in. Another common interest is the aforementioned, almost methodological and metaphysical attention to medicinal apparatuses of bodily research: X-raying, scanning, (virtual) care. Also the rather frequent appearance of signs of what may be interpreted as the cataclysmic and post-supernatural, belonging beyond the laws of nature but almost normalized, associated with liminal spaces of (exo) bodily transition—various hospital spaces, inner cavities. In the context of Rožanskaitė's work, certain psychosomatic and material objects, spaces, installations, and so on could be interpreted as polysemous tropes that stand for mysterious re-articulations of the world, possibly referring to pregnancy, also for shaping, transforming, struggling, and experiencing: metaphysically, aesthetically, spatially, sexually, materially, politically, and otherwise. One of her aims as an artist was to inquire as to whether and how

5   https://www.pakuihardware.org/index.php?/ugnius-gelguda-with-neringa-cerniauskaite/thrivers-polansky-gallery-prague/.
6   https://www.carliergebauer.com/exhibitions/absent_touch.
7   http://www.pakuihardware.org/index.php?/ugnius-gelguda-with-neringa-cerniauskaite/virtual-care-baltic-uk-2021/.
8   https://www.lndm.lt/pakui-hardware-uzdegimas/?lang=en.

multiple openings and closures may activate depicted subjects and audiences. Thought at the time to criticize and reinvent modernism, they also function perfectly nowadays. Thus, the openings could also operate as some uniting element that refers to hope for change to come, as the states, events, and festivals of transitions like solstice, for example, in traditional societies referred to transformational qualities.

The installation at Sant'Antonin church in Venice, a place that normally serves as a station for belief, community, and transcendence, offers no empty promises that the new, fairer world is about to be born and that the long-overdue inflammation of the world is about to pass. Instead, the installation may be seen as a place for transition, even if the transition is long overdue. Typically, transition is an important part of traditional societies. Baltic pagans, like other Indigenous people, believe in a transition that would connect personal and cosmogonic systems. The archetypal transformations that Indigenous people encounter can be summarized in a nutshell as the interplay between order and chaos. Order and chaos were seen as the oldest characteristics of the world. In most mythologies and scriptures, the creation of the world—order—begins with chaos. According to one of the pagan Lithuanian etiologic (belonging to studies of causation) stories, the first humans were created from a god's spit into the sea, coming out as a piece of dribbling foam. God spat and went away.

Humans since then have been trying to survive in this not-very-hospitable environment. For Baltic and other tribes, meaning and harmony were constantly reestablished through rituals, practices, and feasts connected to transitional moments on the calendar, like summer and winter solstices. The transitional periods were meant to be of extreme importance, as the transition was understood as a phenomenon that we were constantly confronted with in daily life. This (body) shifting, an in-between stage, was seen as a general and all-encompassing phenomenon. Every transformation, no matter how large or small, was seen as a repetition of the great transformation—the (re)creation of the world. And although

we, inflamed, today may feel or seem to be abandoned, exploited carcasses with the surplus of life and well-being ripped from our lives, the installation serves as a reminder of where we've been together already for centuries. And this is why it may be possible to see the presentation, this intergenerational techno-organism, as a station of shared inflammation that at the end, at least speculatively, indicates a possible healing and hope.

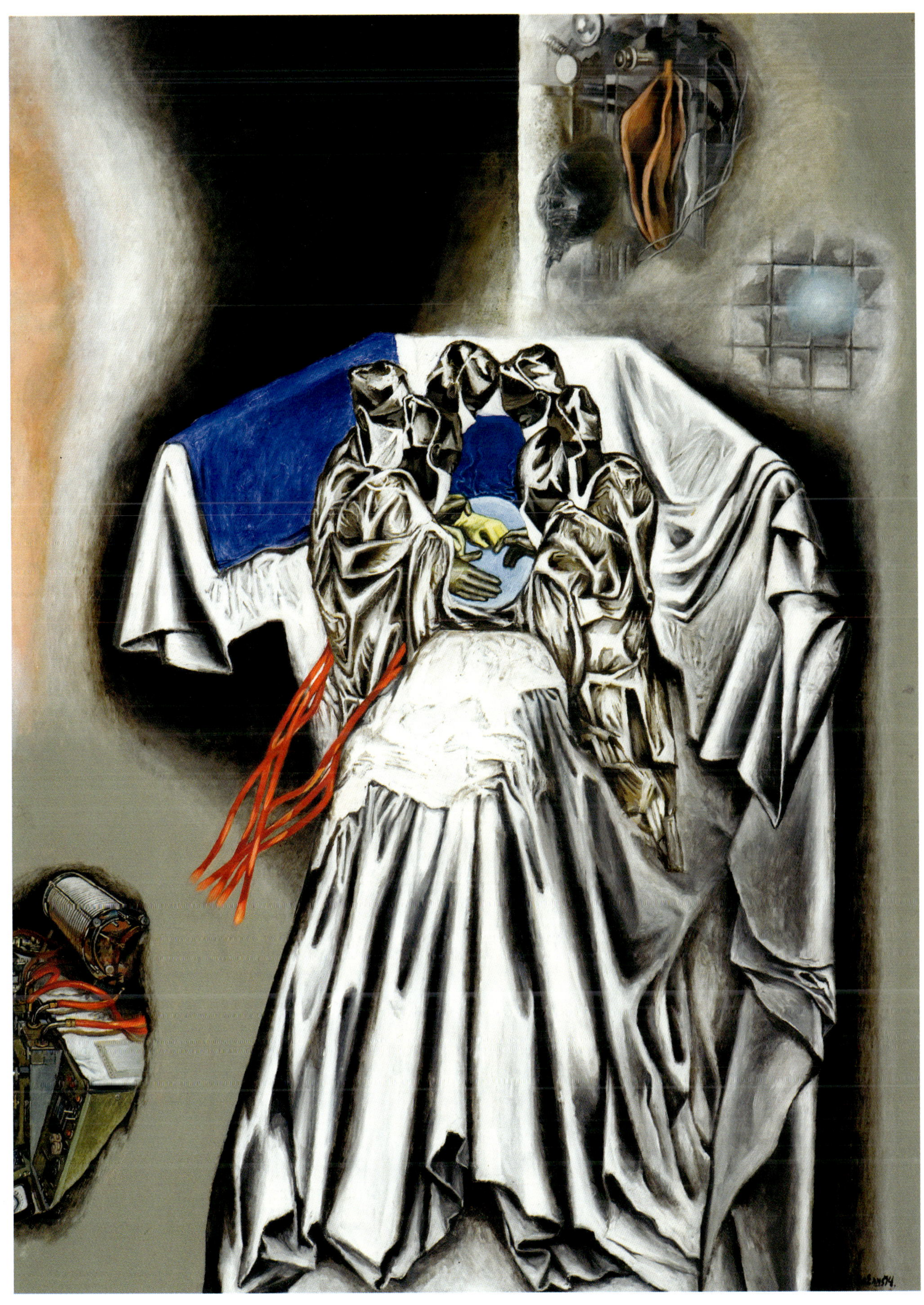

21 ↑ Marija Teresė Rožanskaitė, *Heart Surgery*, 1974. Oil on cardboard, 240 × 170 cm
Photo: Antanas Lukšėnas. Courtesy the Lithuanian National Museum of Art, Vilnius

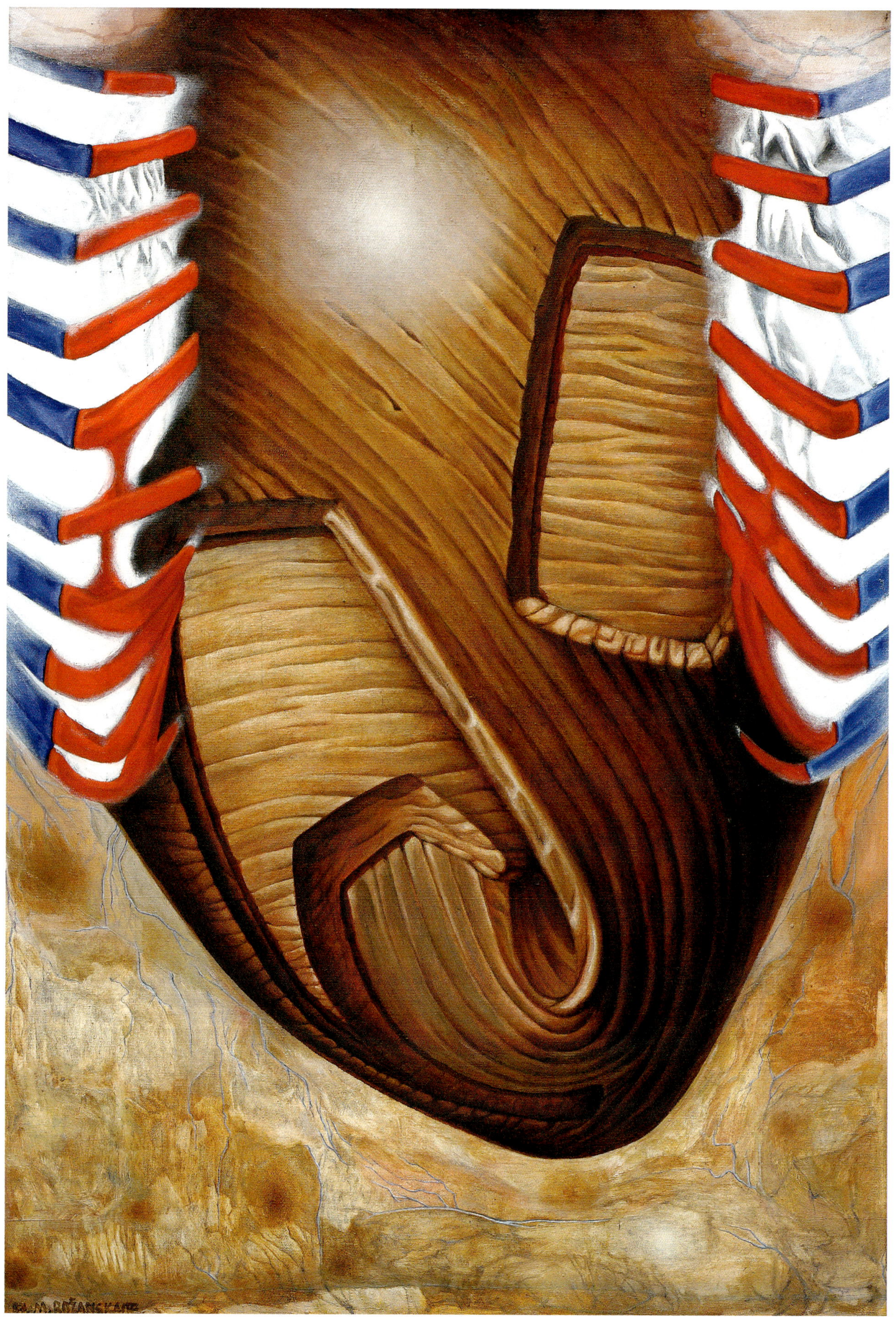

↑ Marija Teresė Rožanskaitė, *Heart*, 1987. Oil on canvas, 130 × 90 cm
Photo: Vidmantas Ilčiukas. Courtesy the artist's family

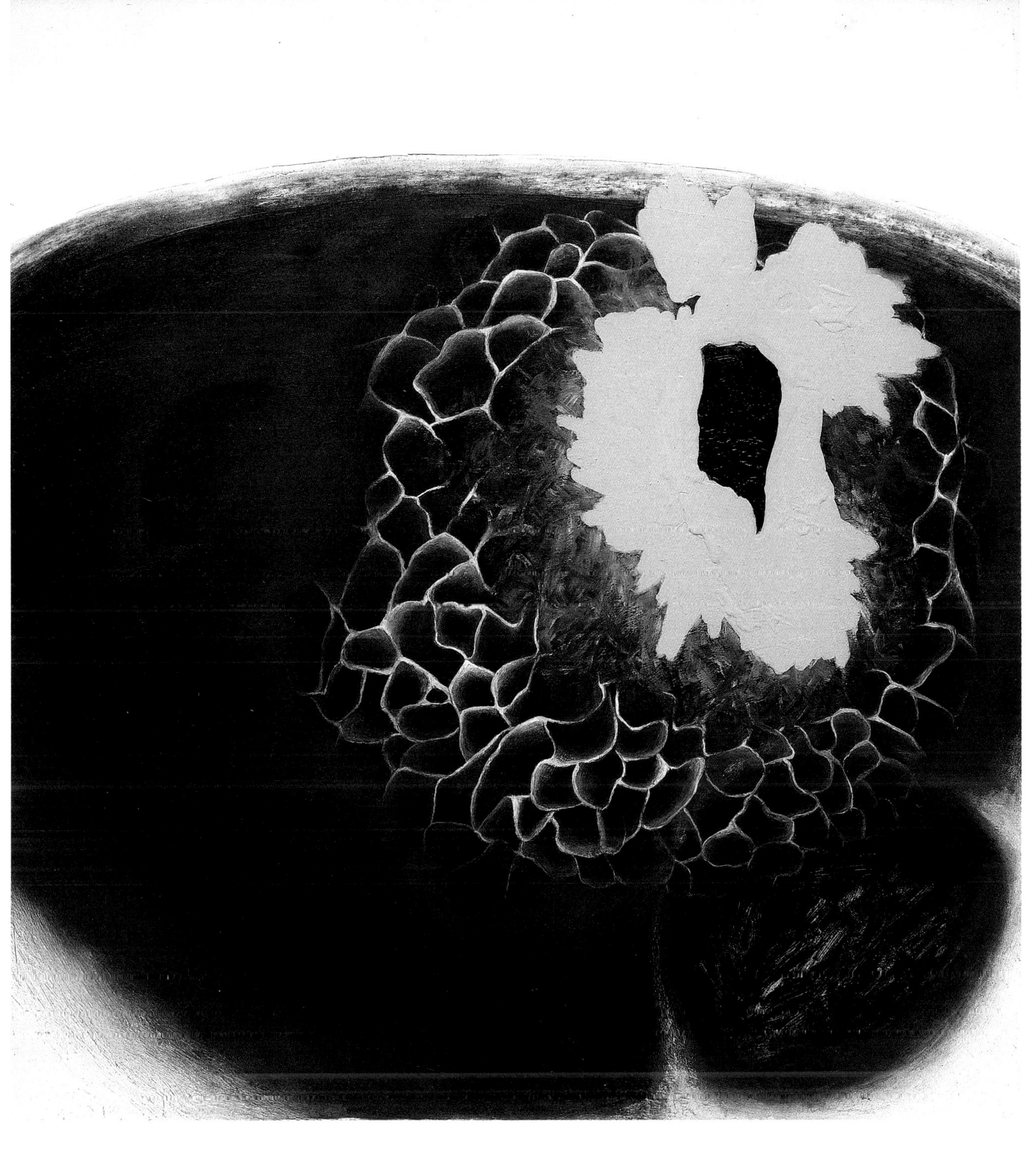

 ↑   Marija Teresė Rožanskaitė, *Cosmic Composition*, 1979. Oil on cardboard, 122 × 105 cm
Photo: Vidmantas Ilčiukas. Courtesy the artist's family

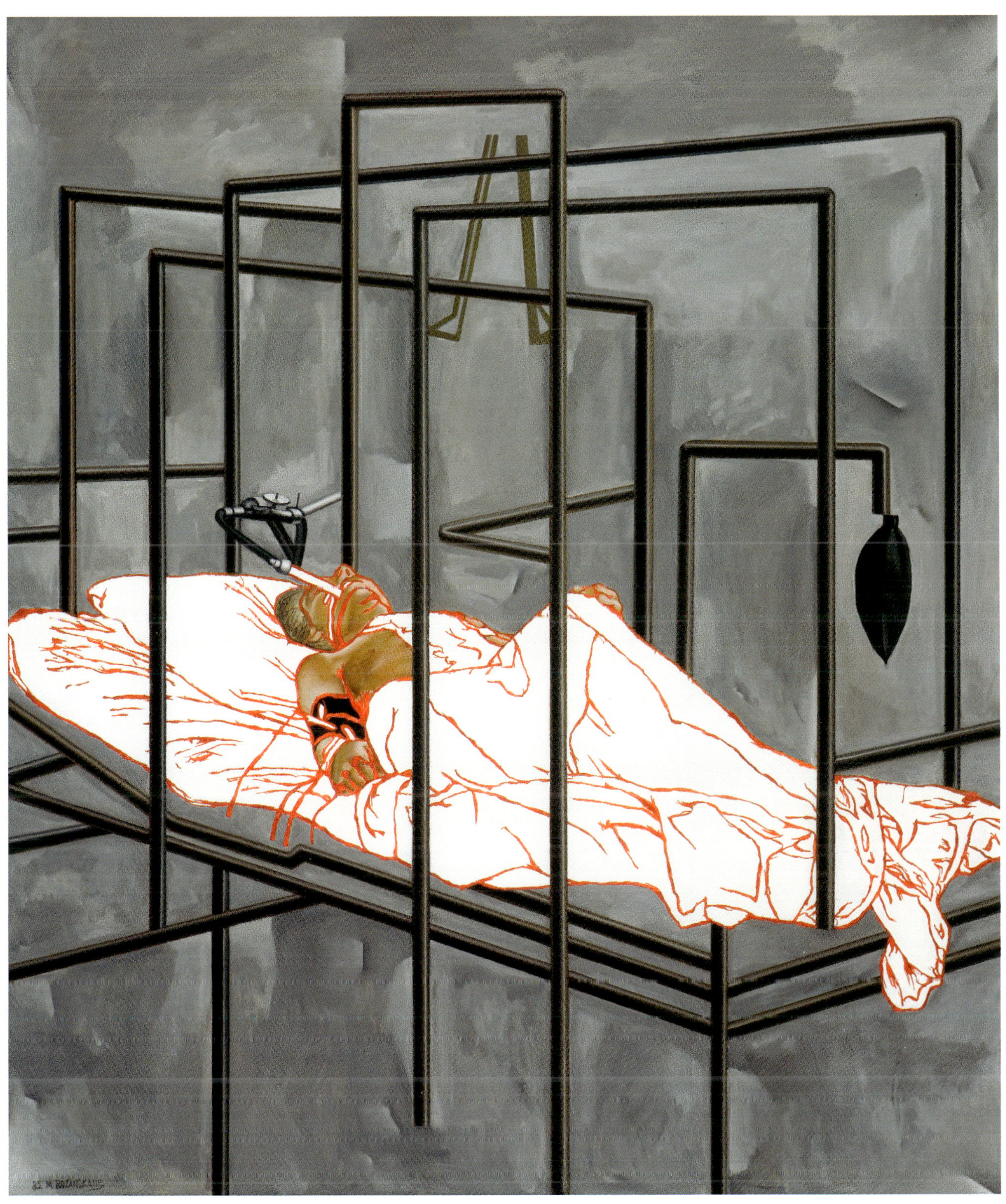

25 ↑   Marija Teresė Rožanskaitė, *Disease*, 1985. Oil on canvas, 150 × 130 cm
Photo. Antanas Lukšėnas. Courtesy the Lithuanian National Museum of Art, Vilnius

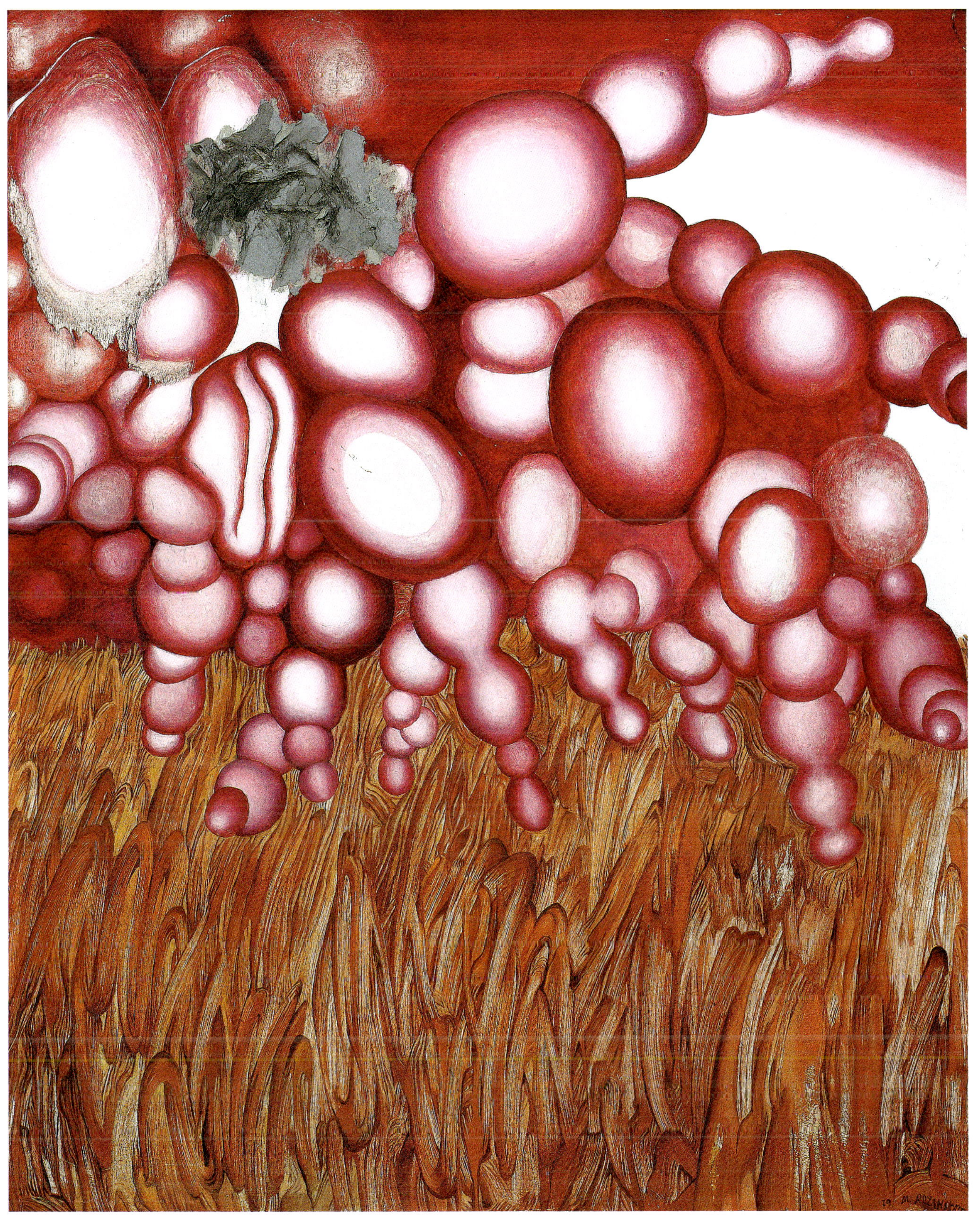

↑ Marija Teresė Rožanskaitė, *Fantastic Composition*, 1979. Oil on cardboard, 115 × 105 cm
Photo. Vidmantas Ilčiukas. Courtesy the artist's family

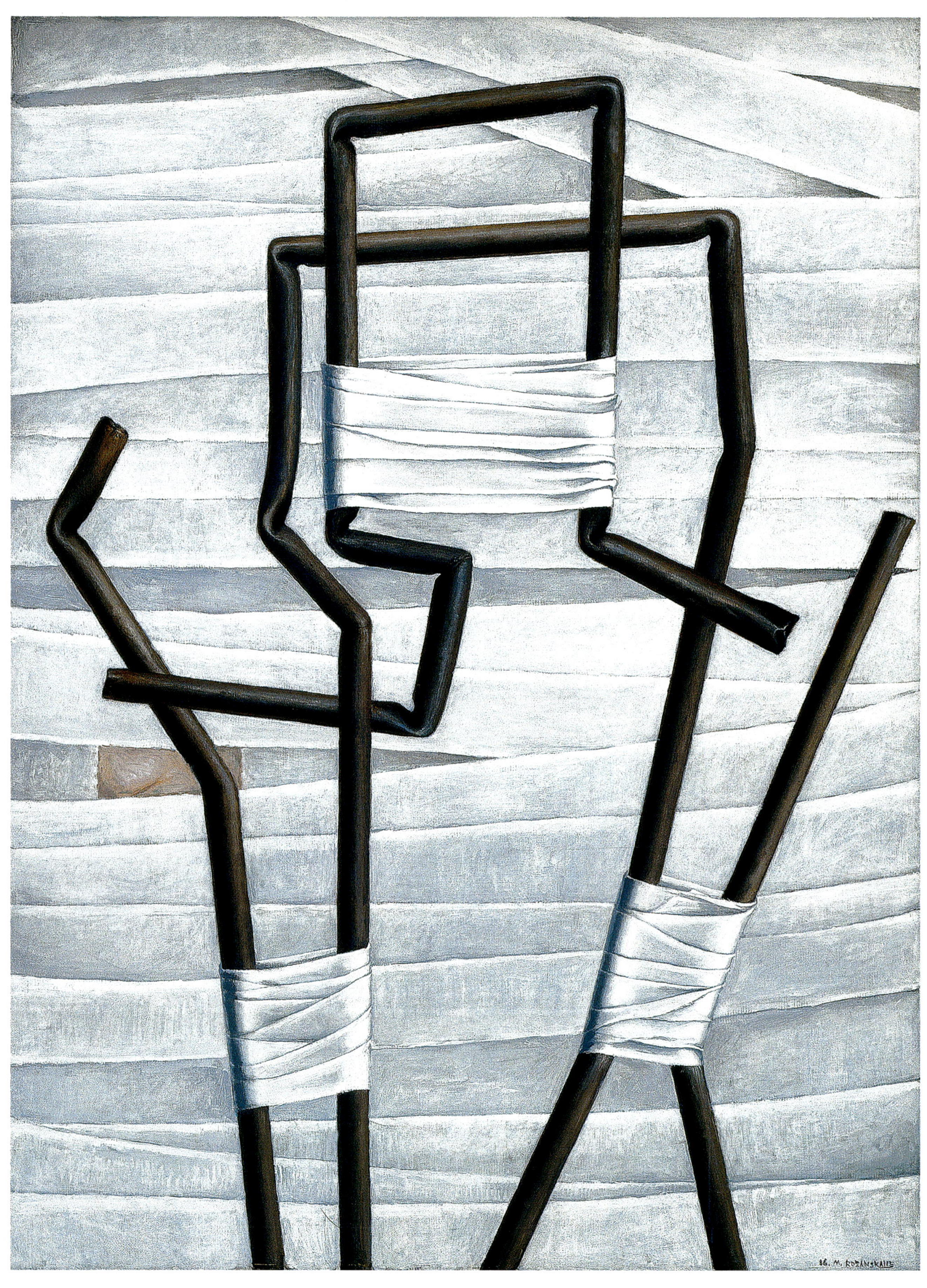

↑ Marija Teresė Rožanskaitė, *Reinforcement Rods*, 1986. Oil on canvas, 144.5 × 130 cm
Photo: Vidmantas Ilčiukas. Courtesy the artist's family

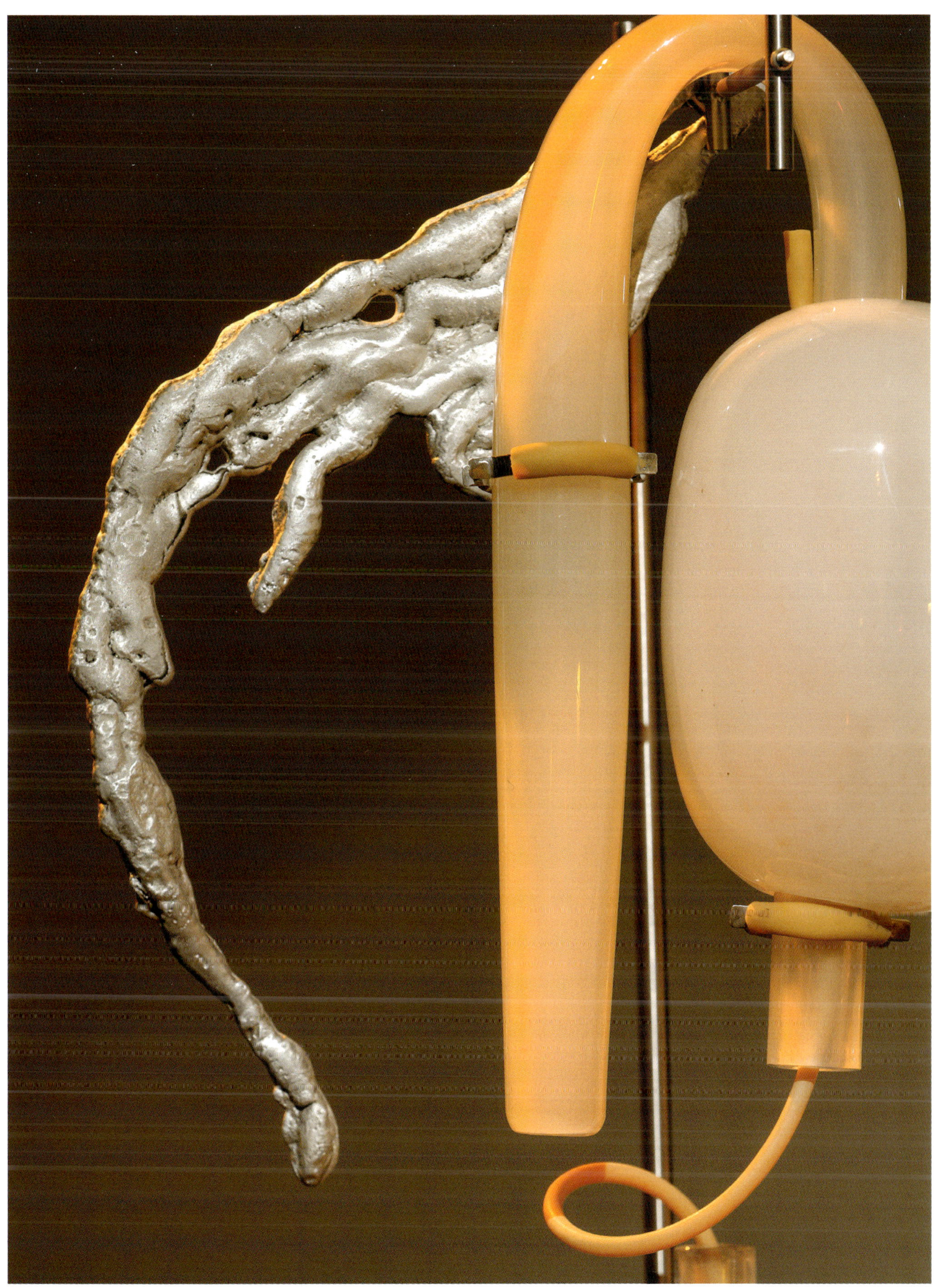

29 ↑→ Pakui Hardware, *Inflammation*, 2023. Installation view, Lithuanian National Museum of Art (Museum of Applied Arts and Design), 2023
Photo: Ugnius Gelguda. Courtesy the artists, the Lithuanian National Museum of Art, and carlier | gebauer, Berlin & Madrid

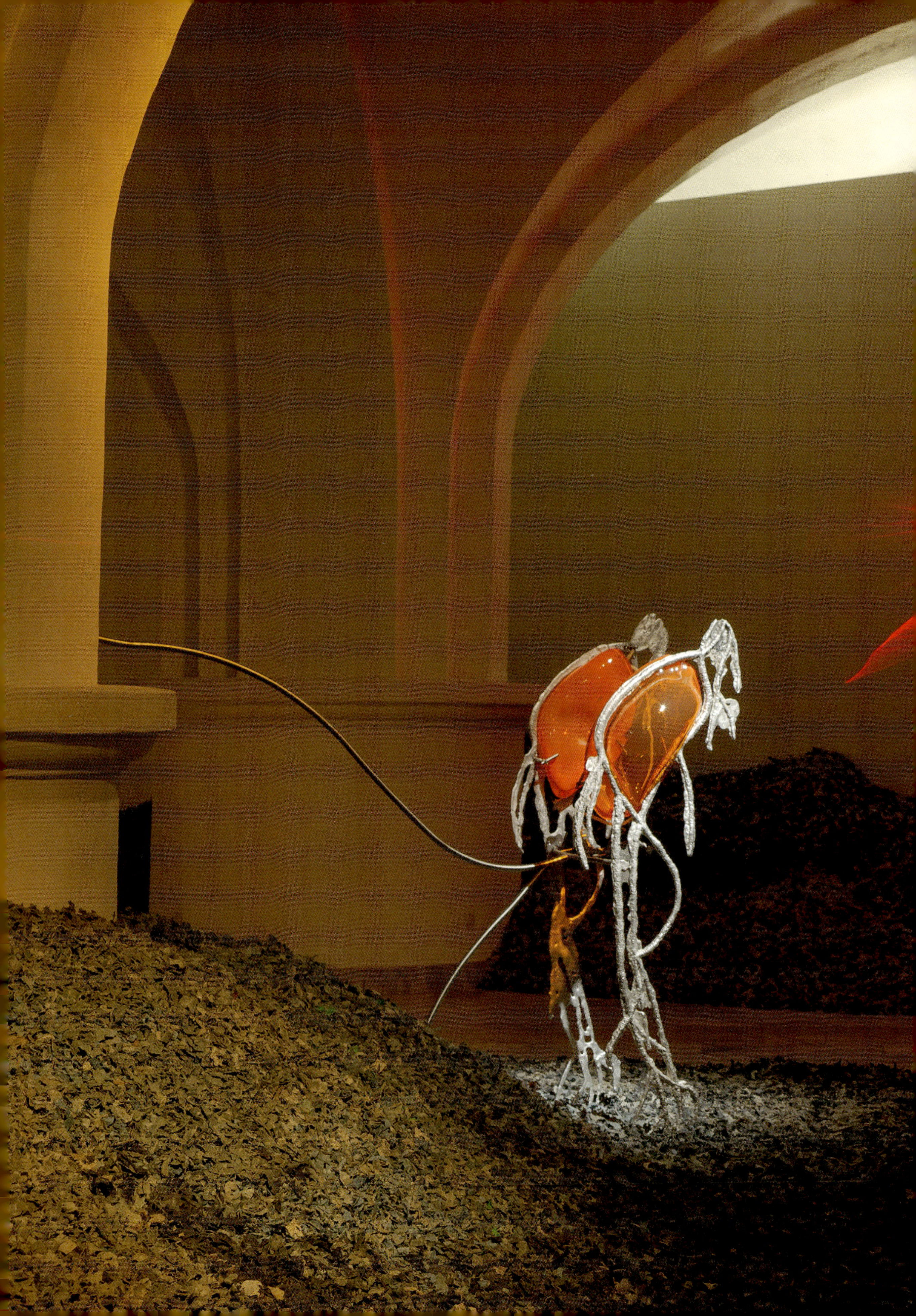

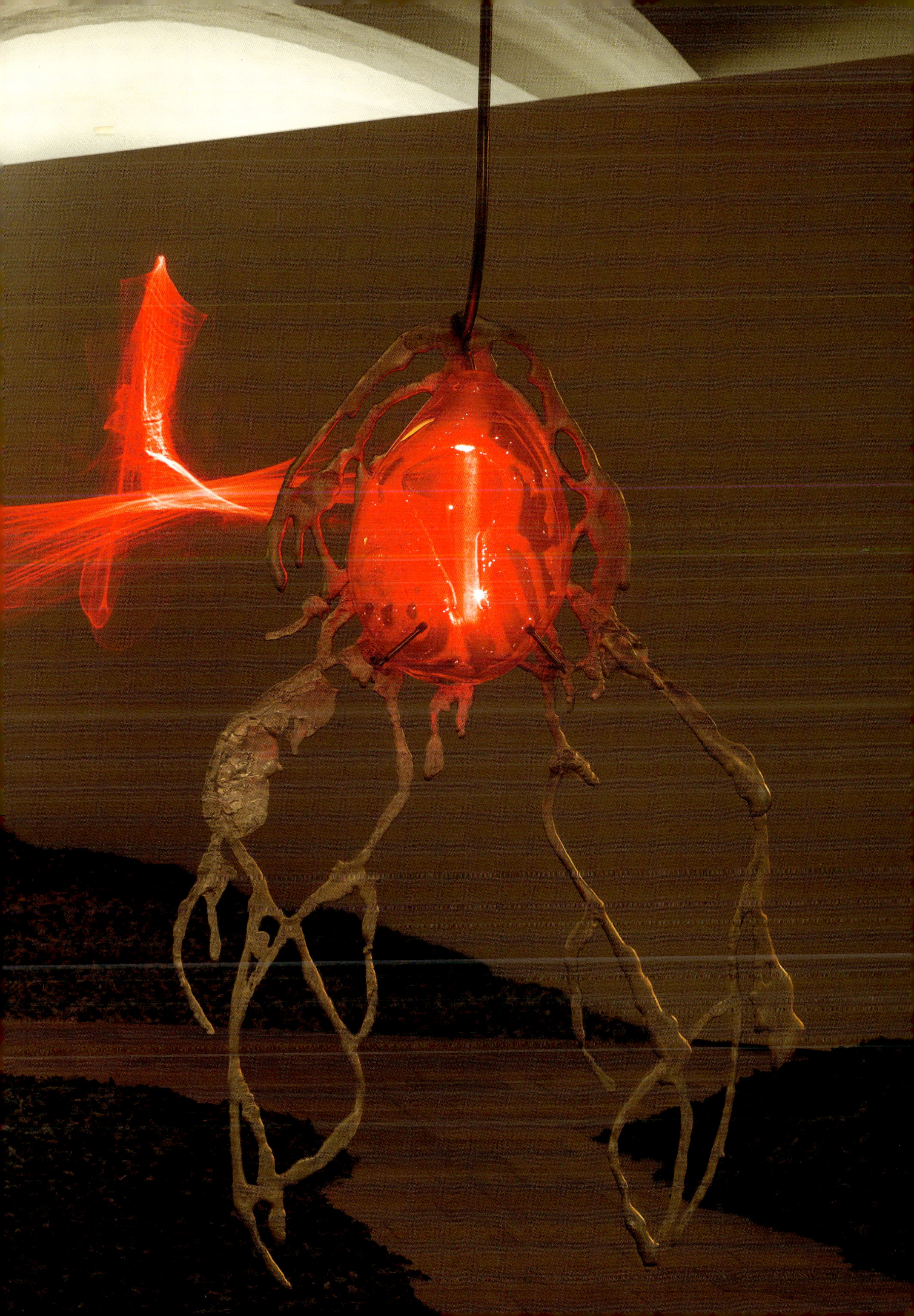

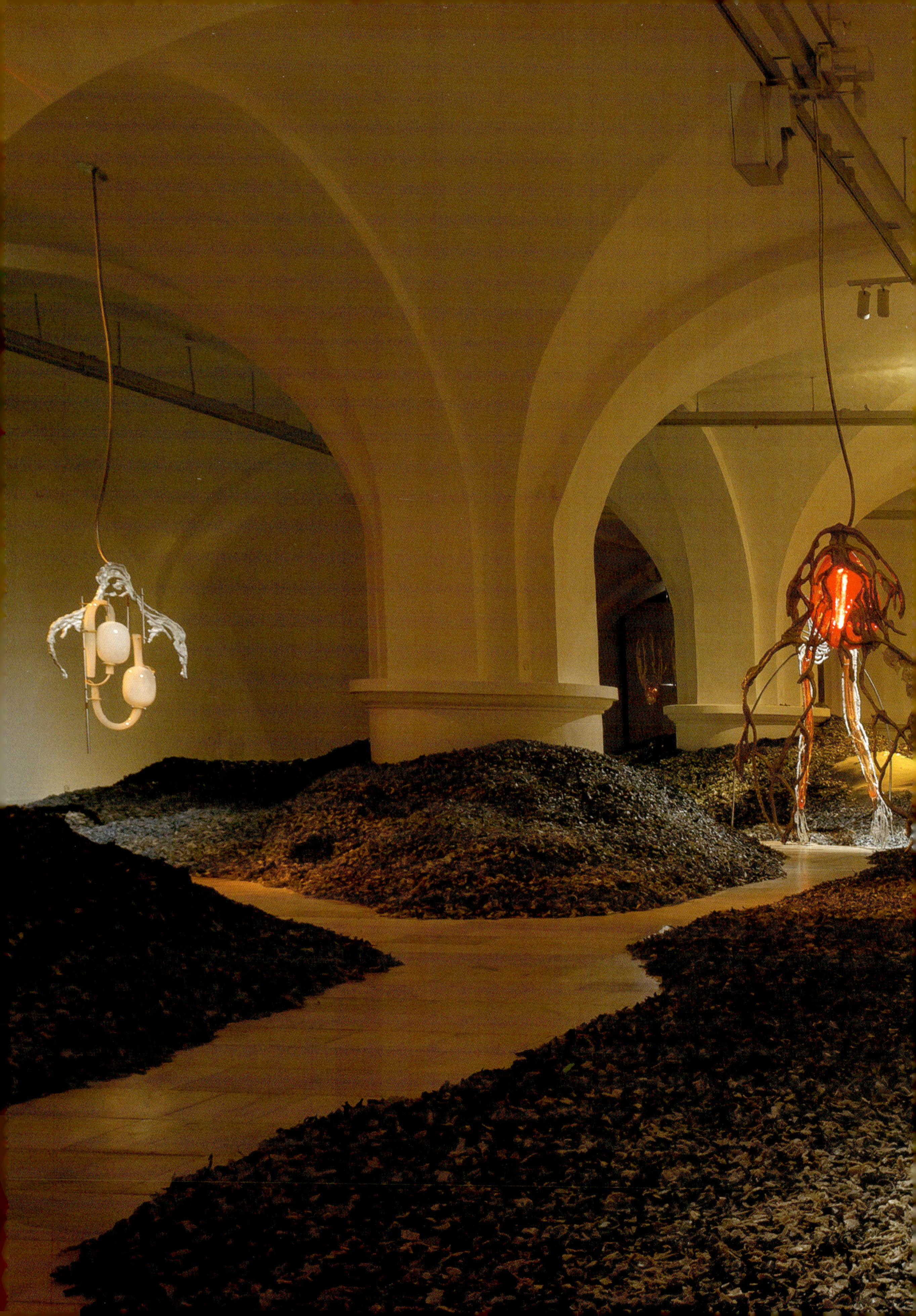

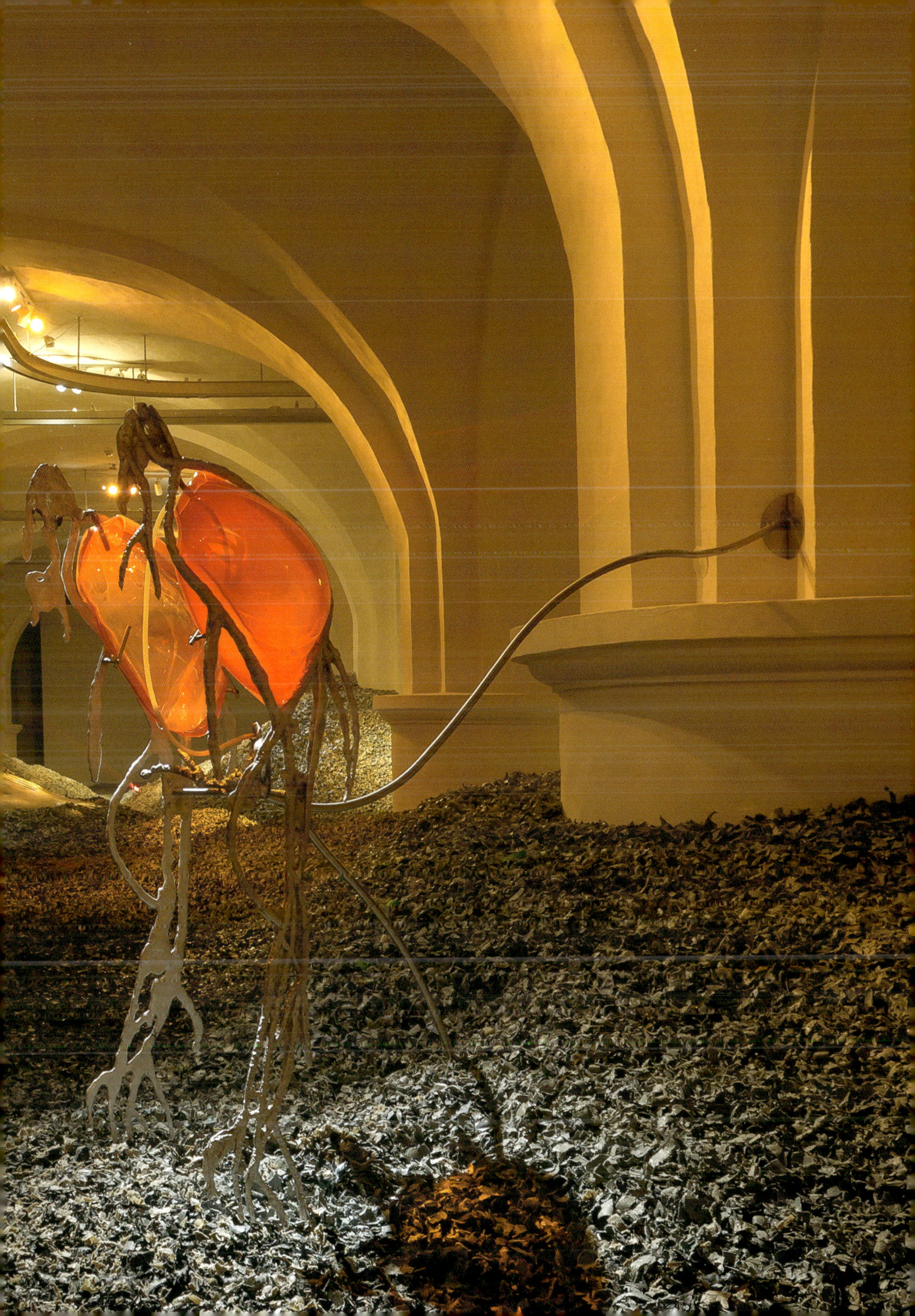

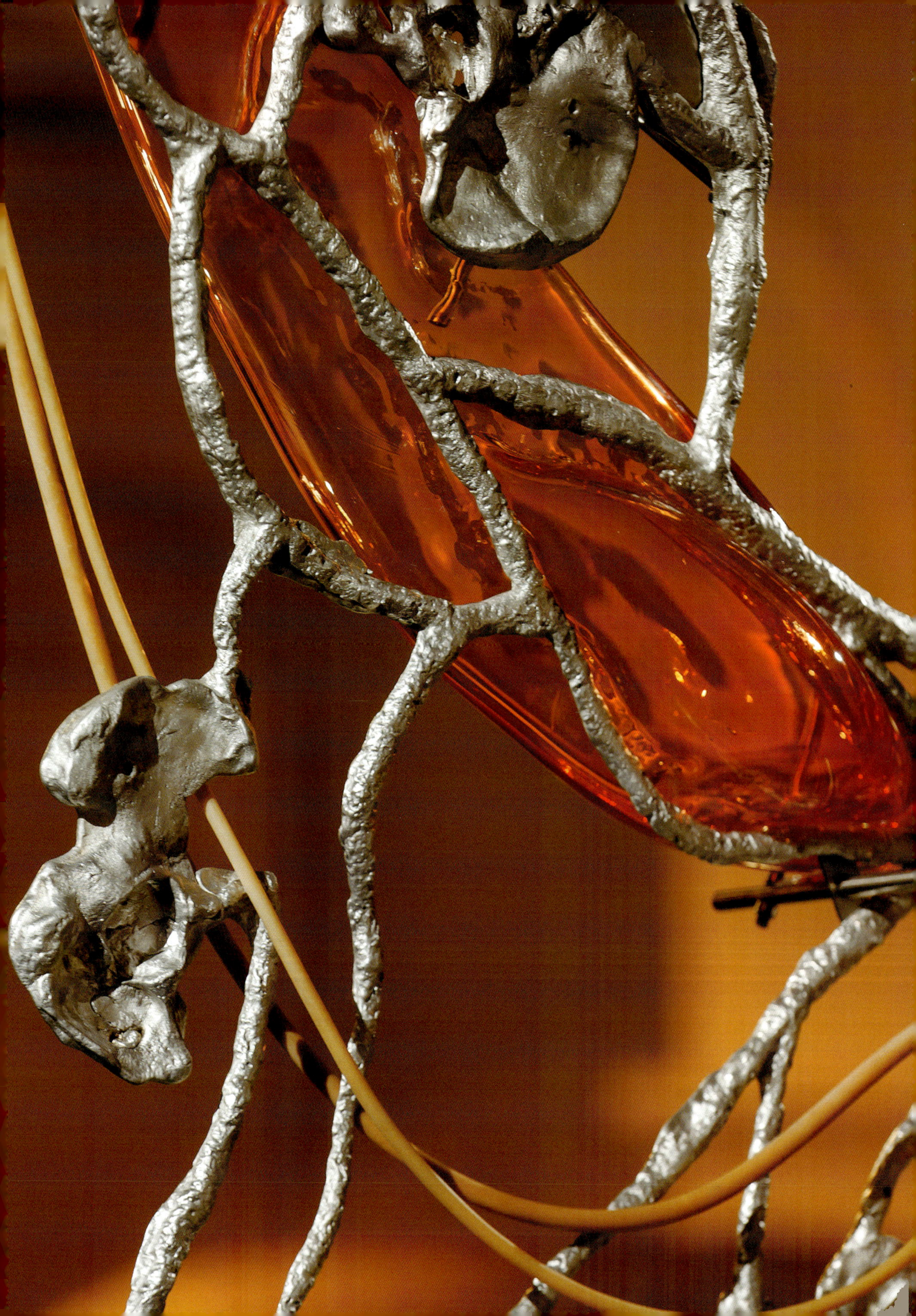

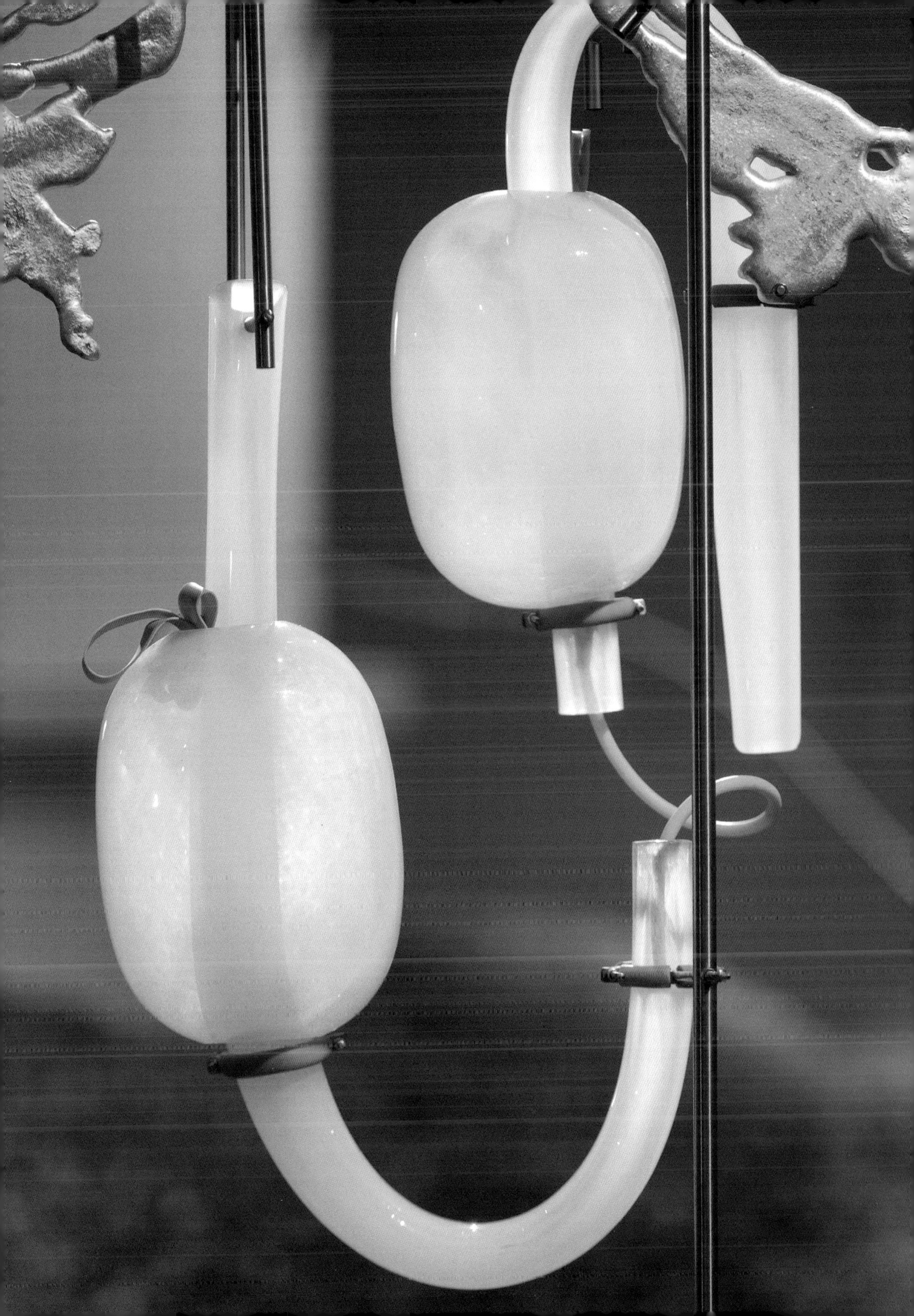

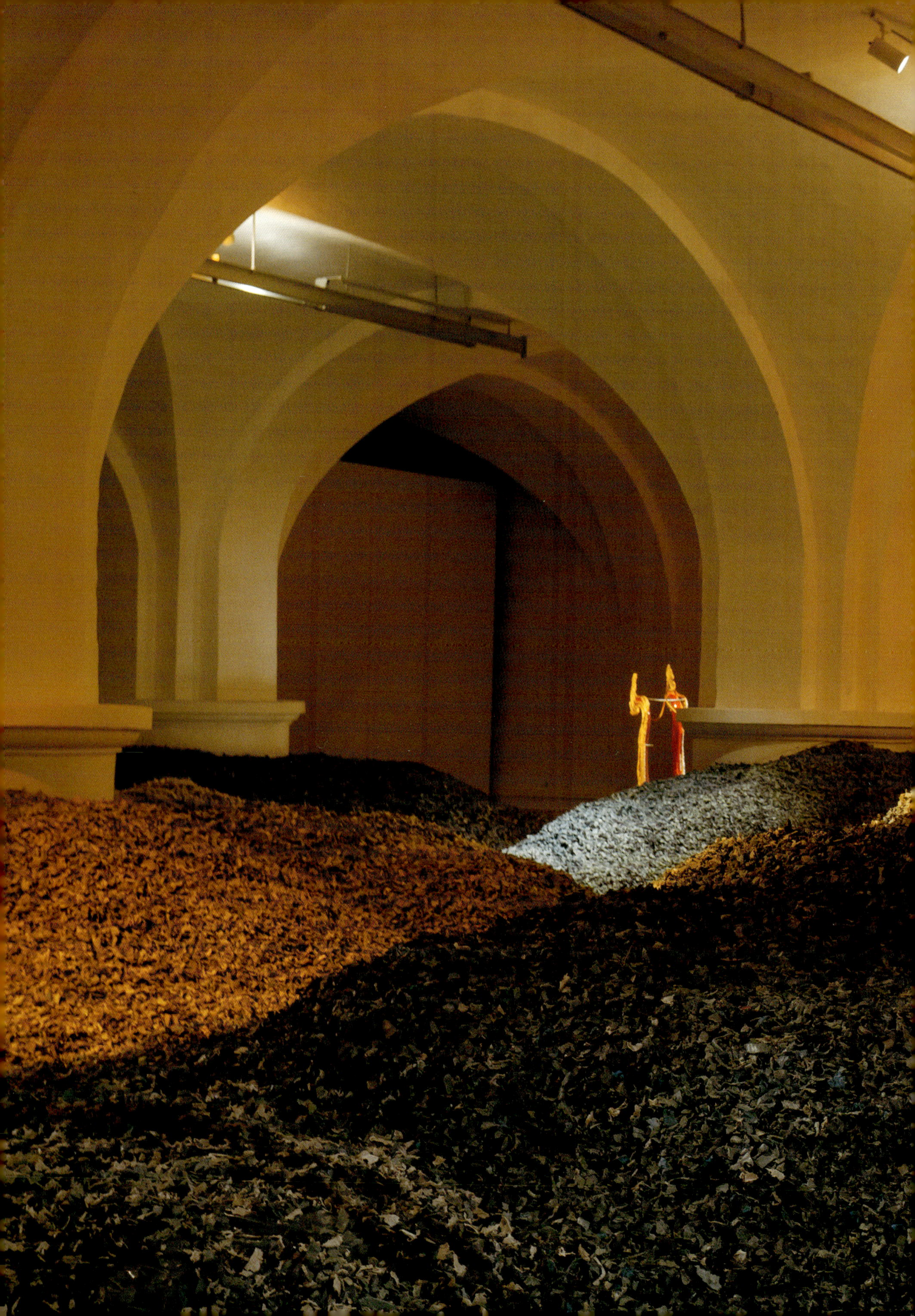

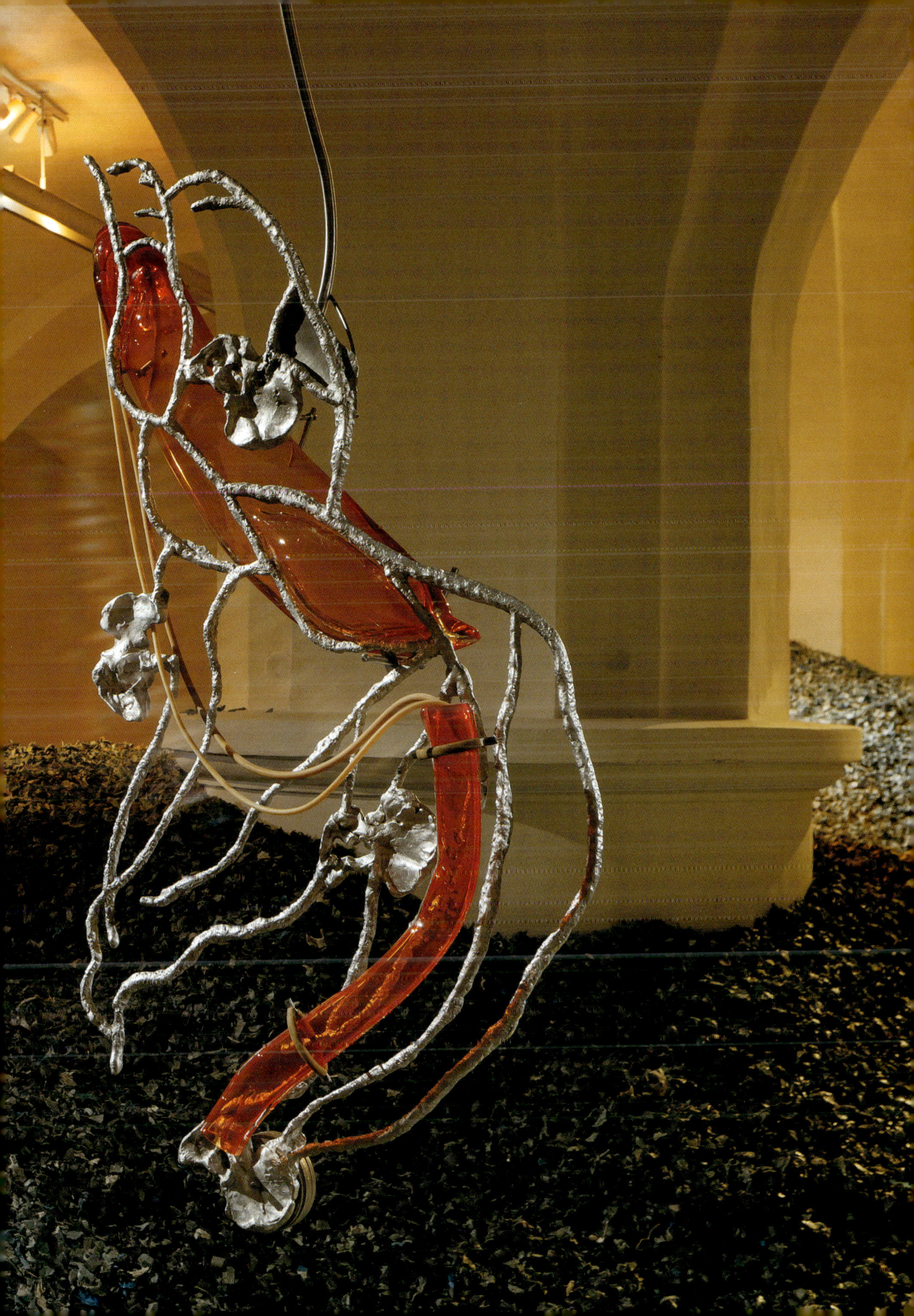

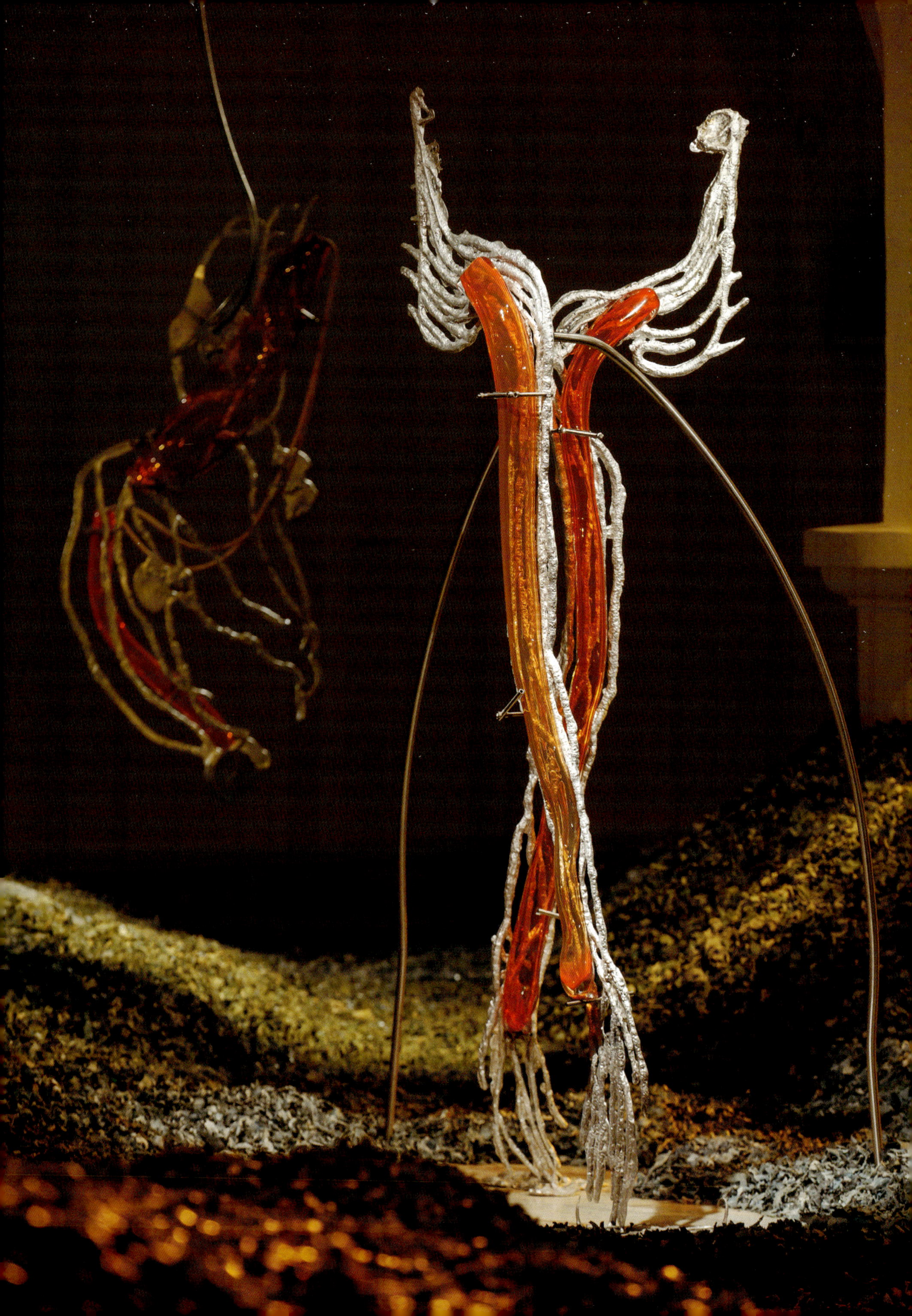

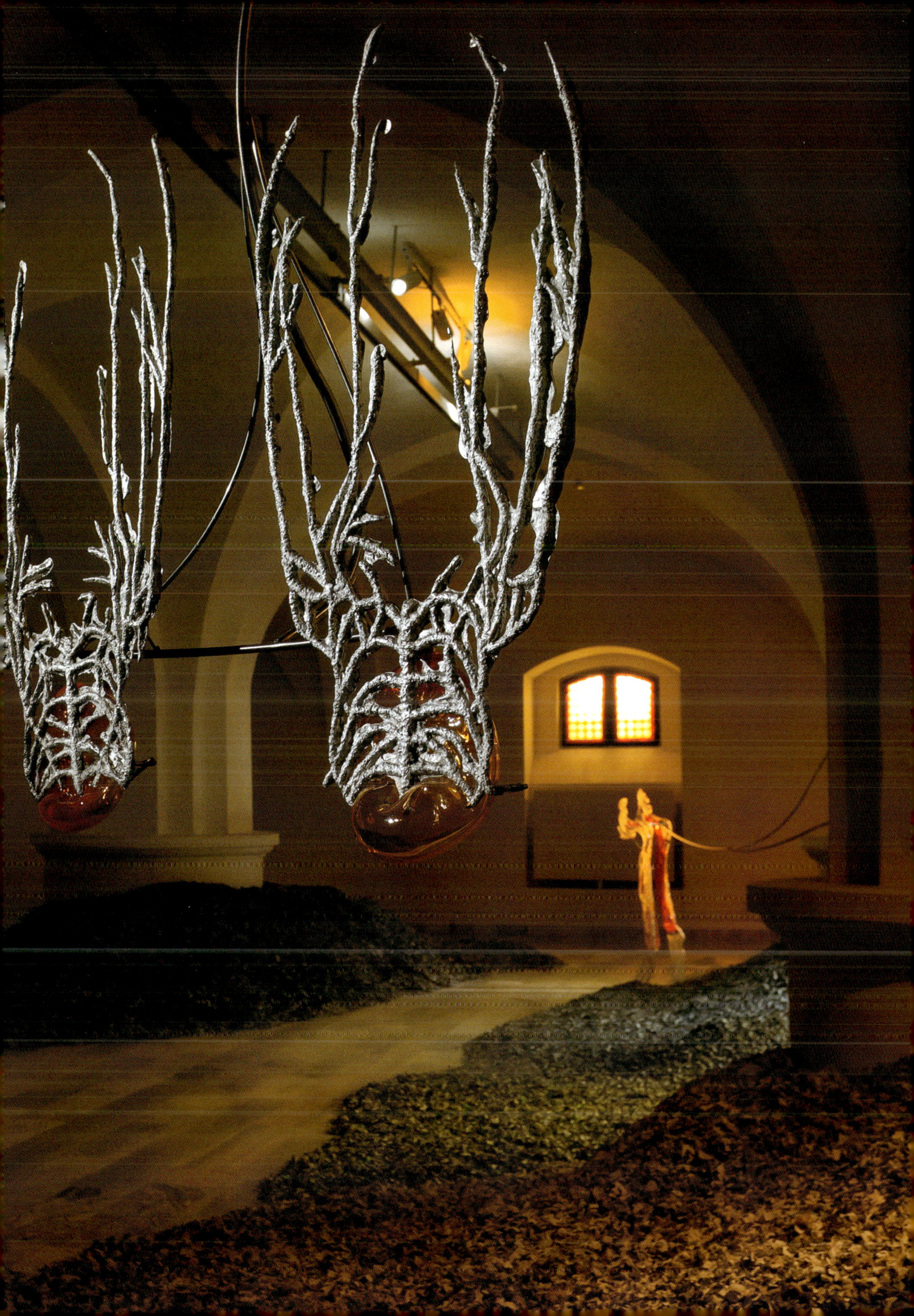

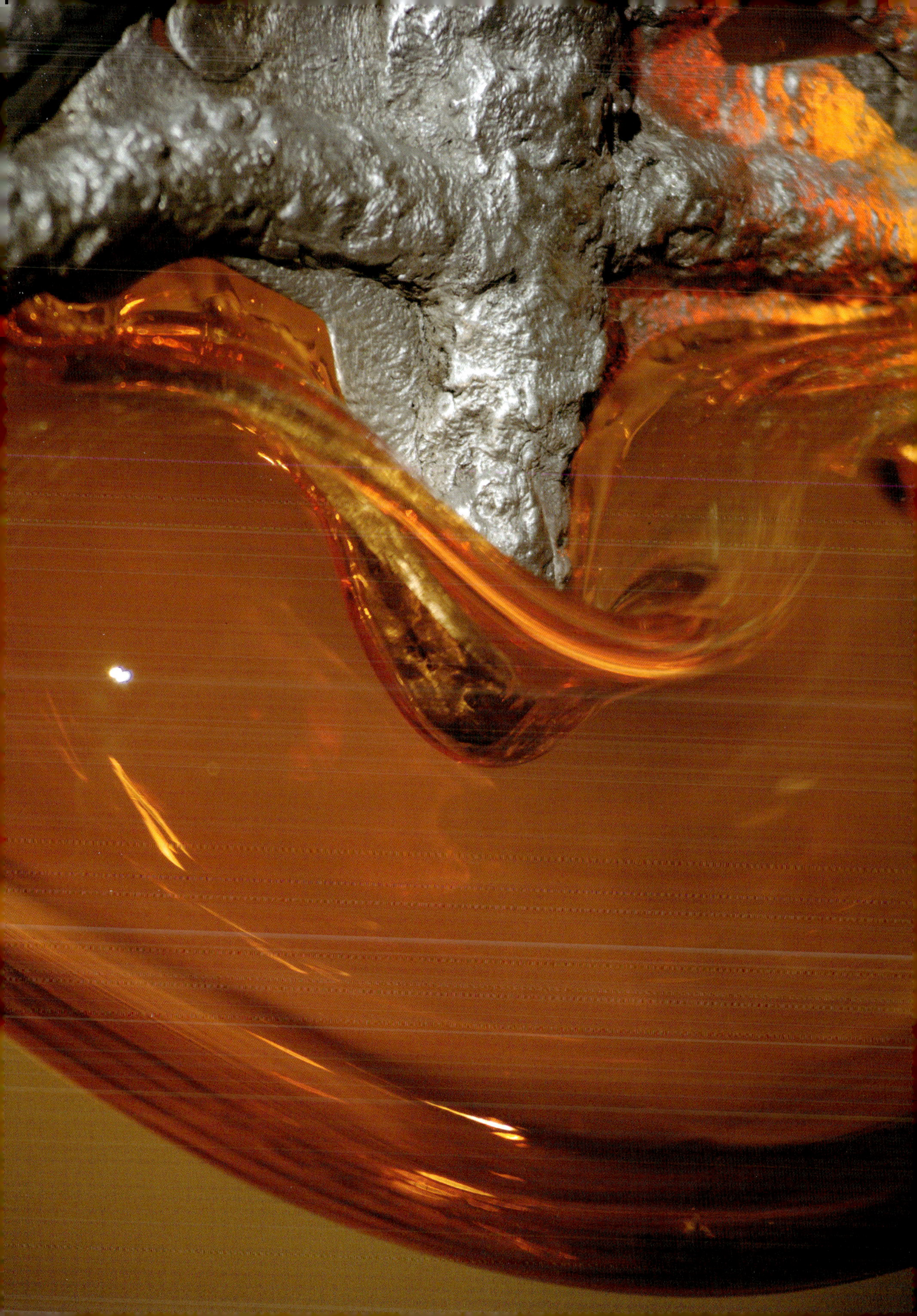

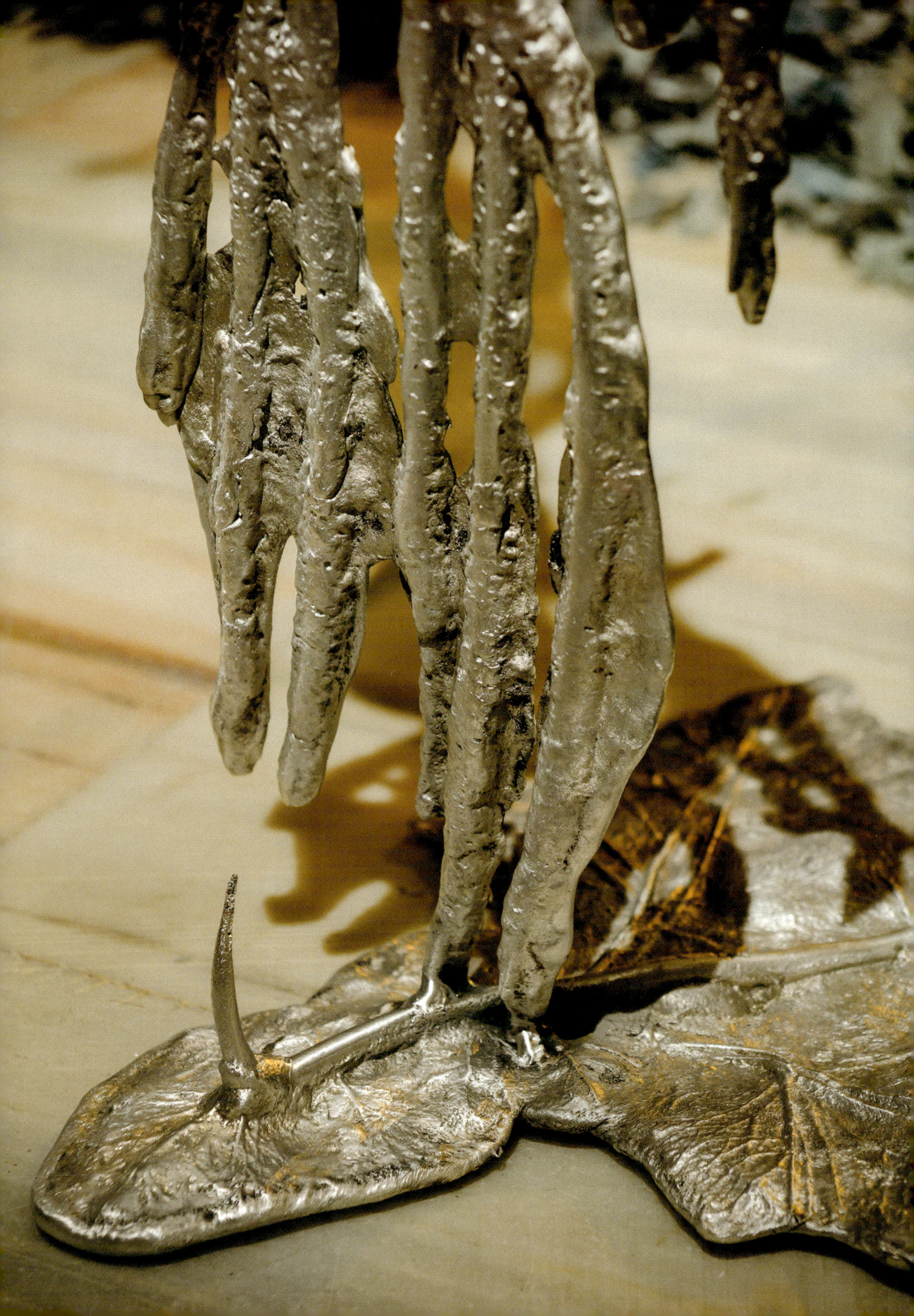

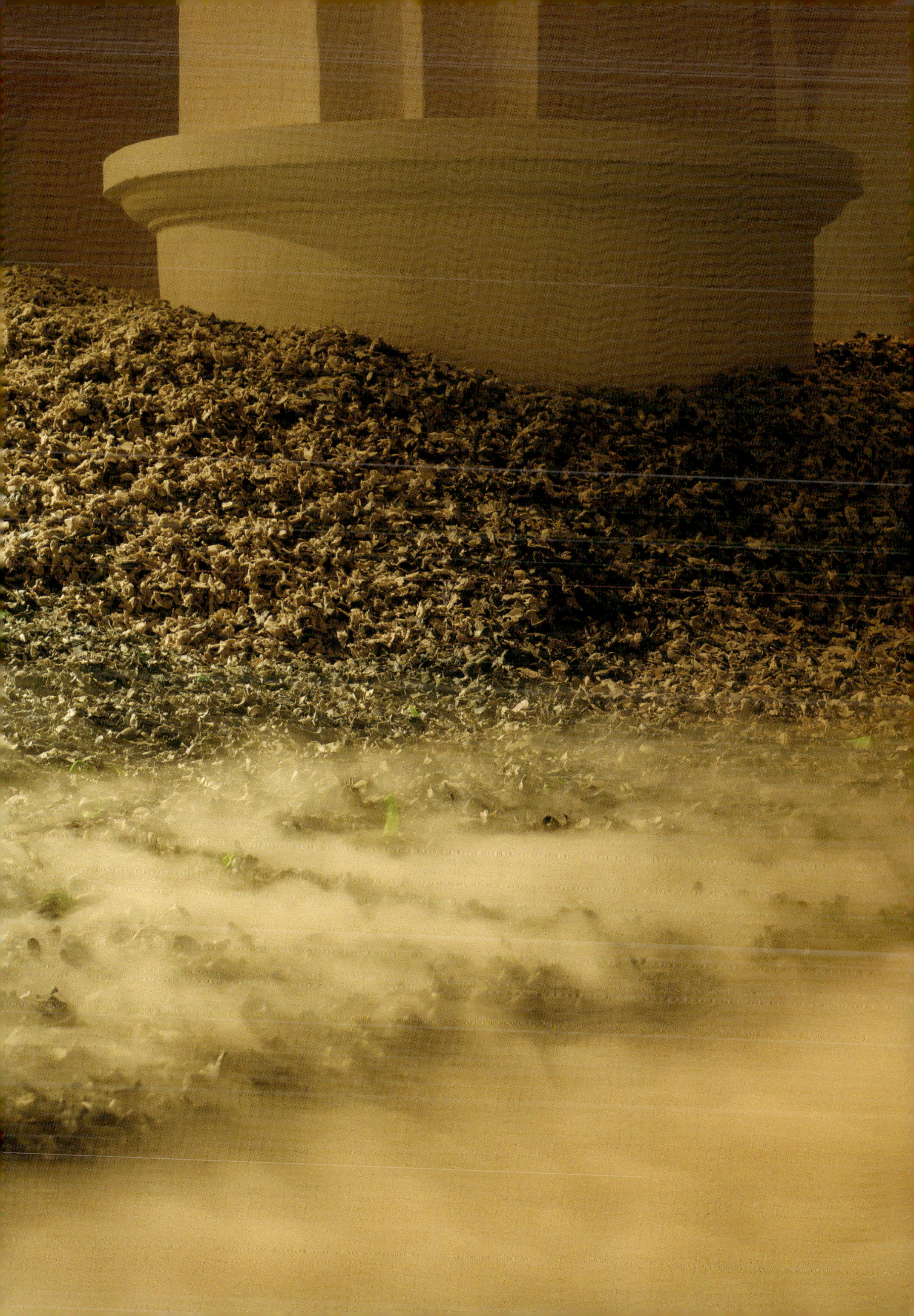

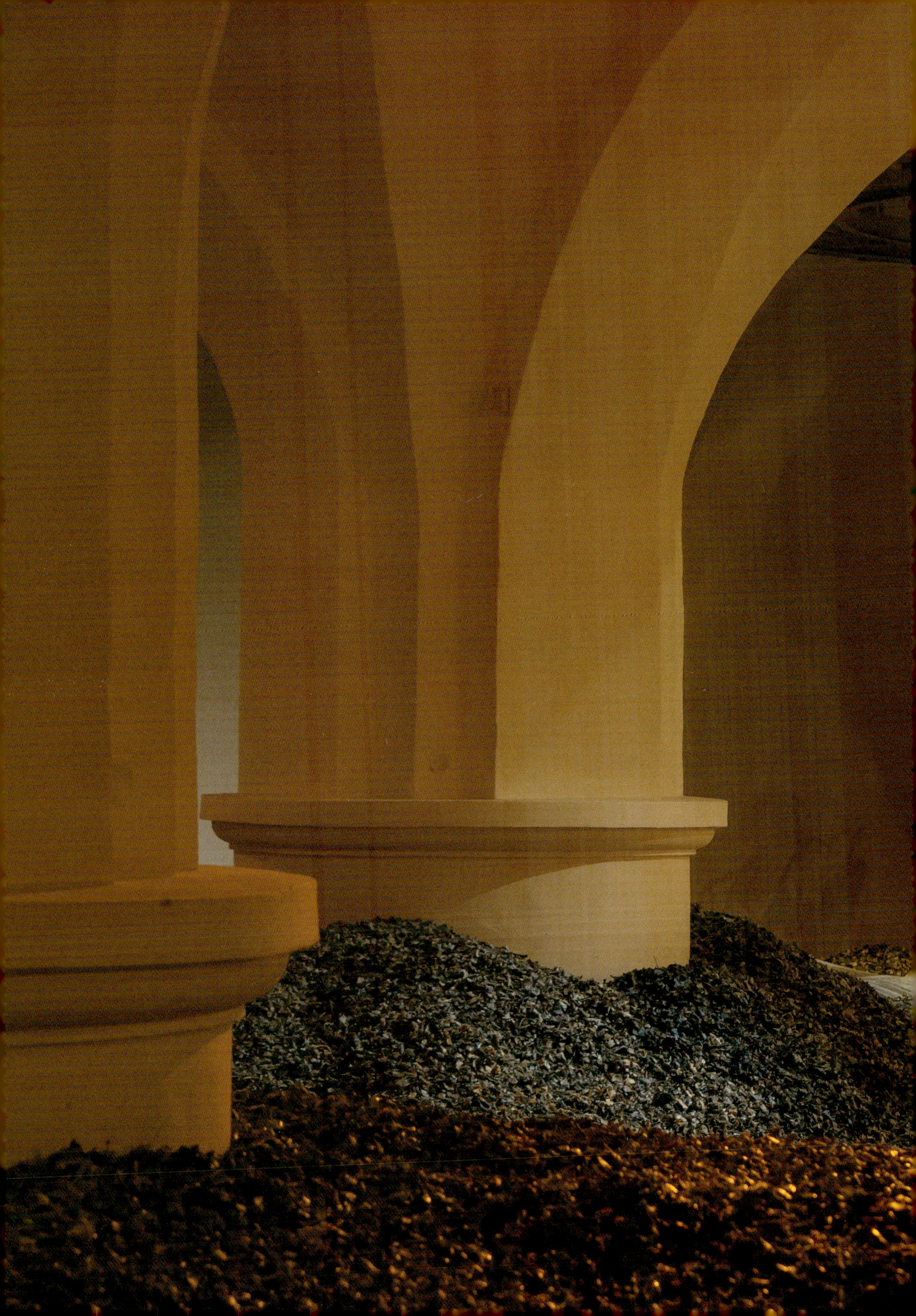

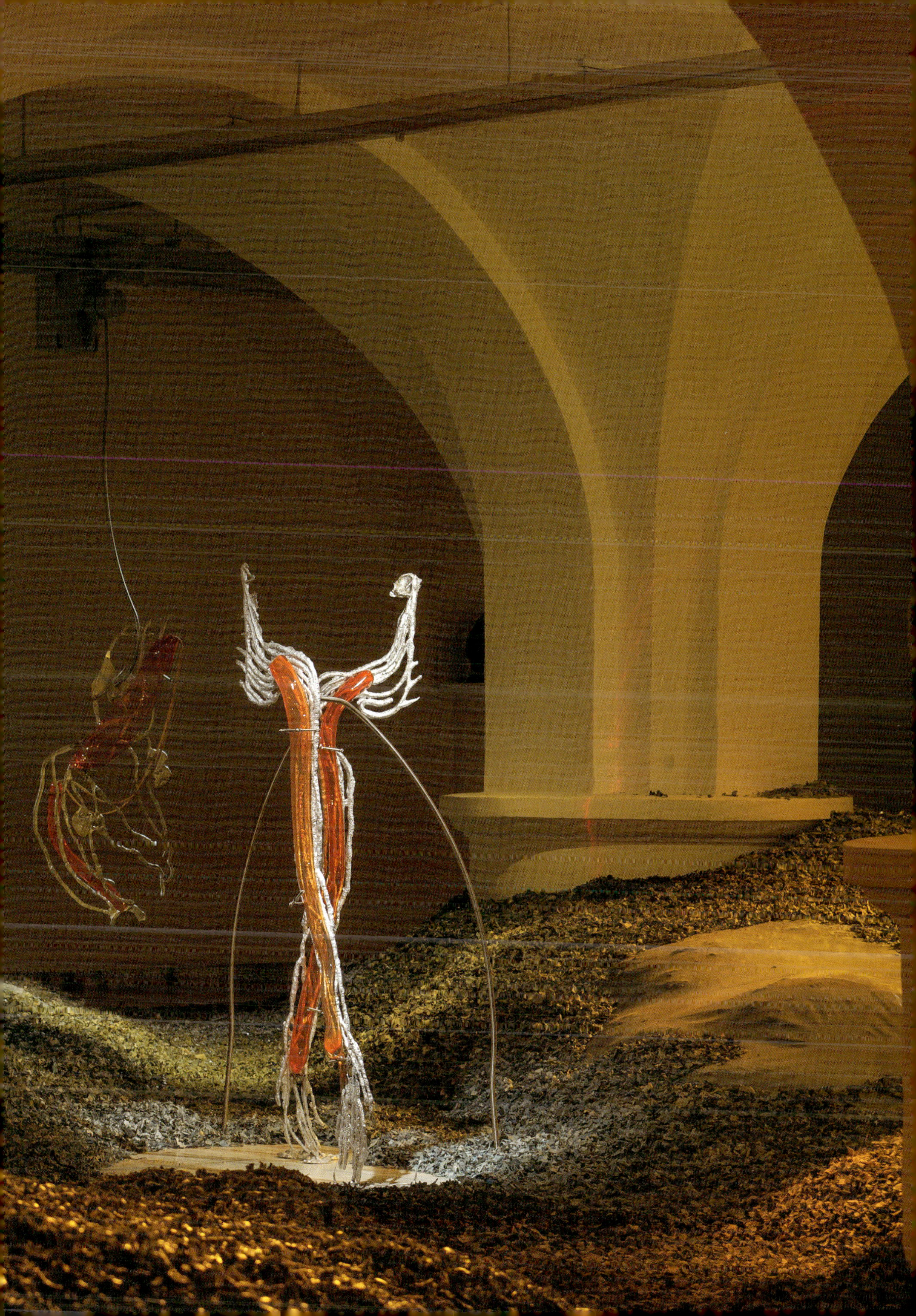

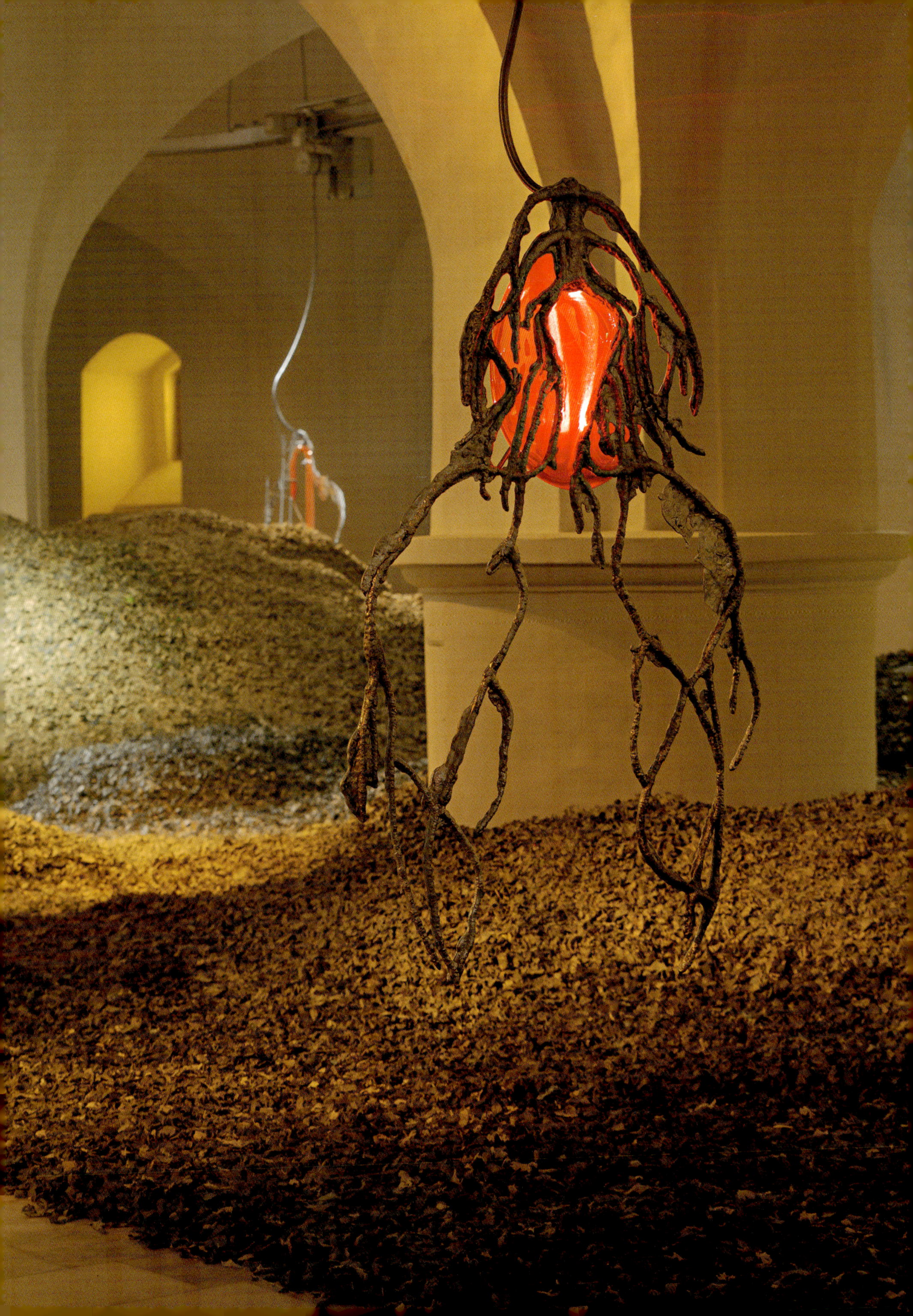

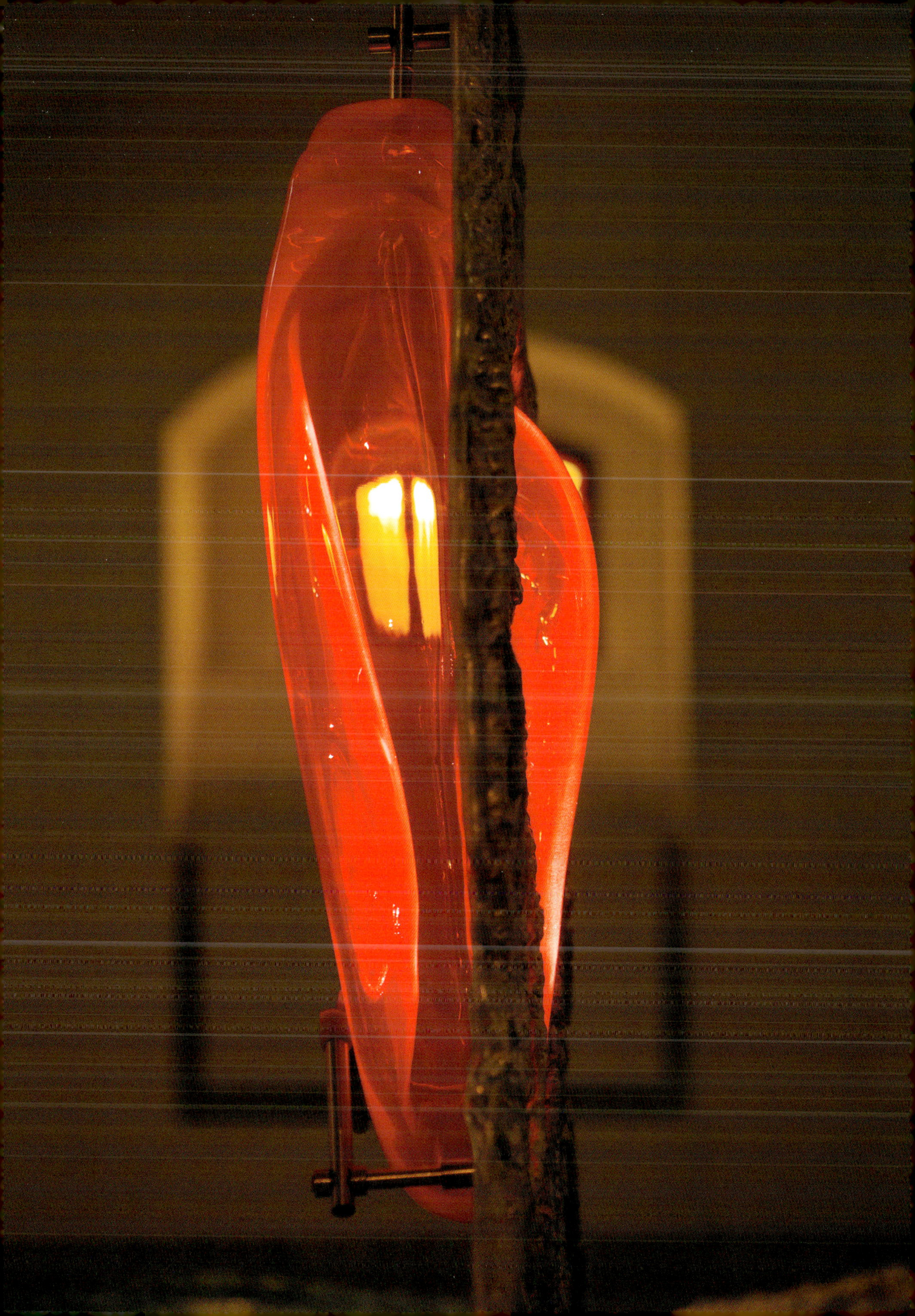

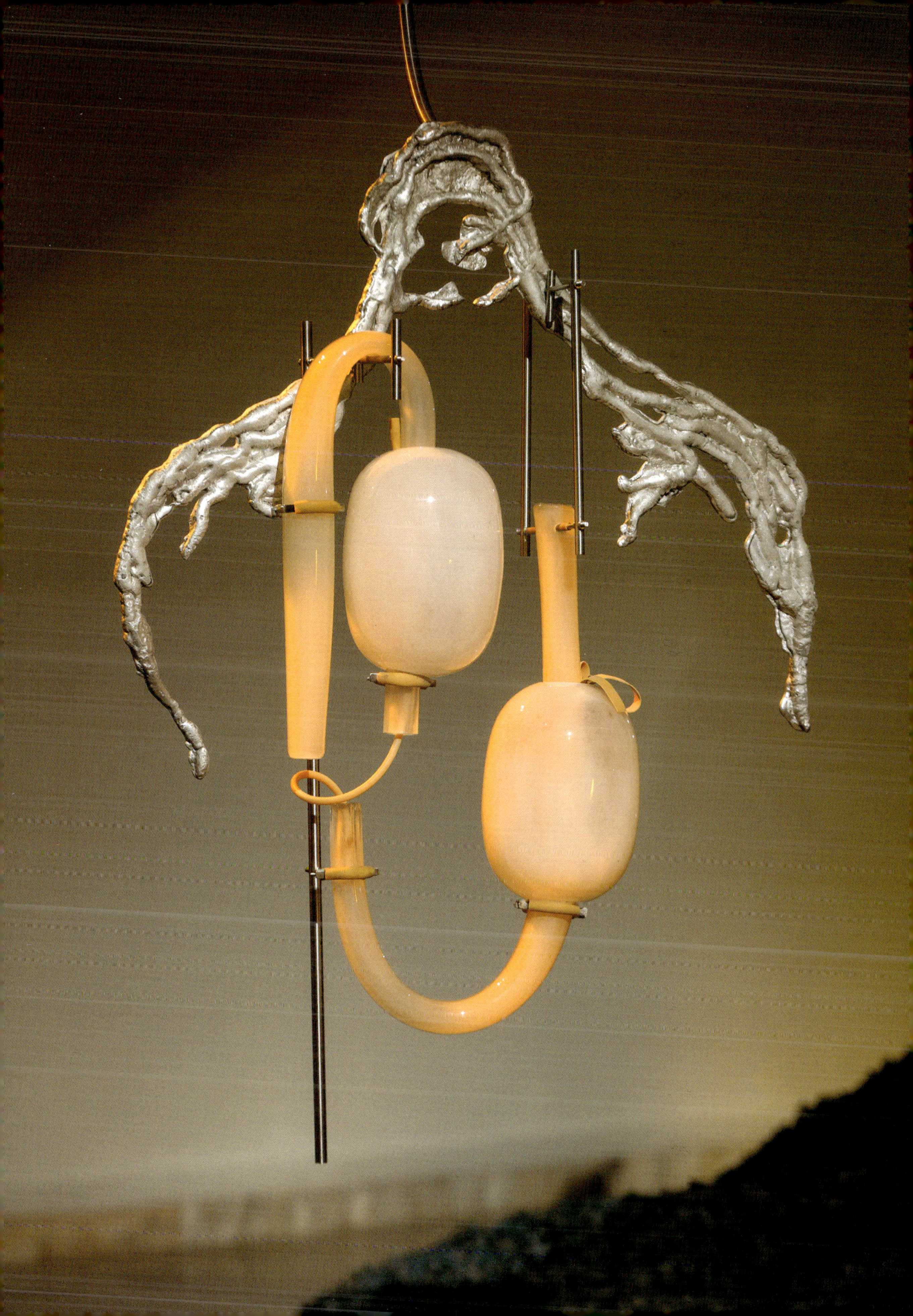

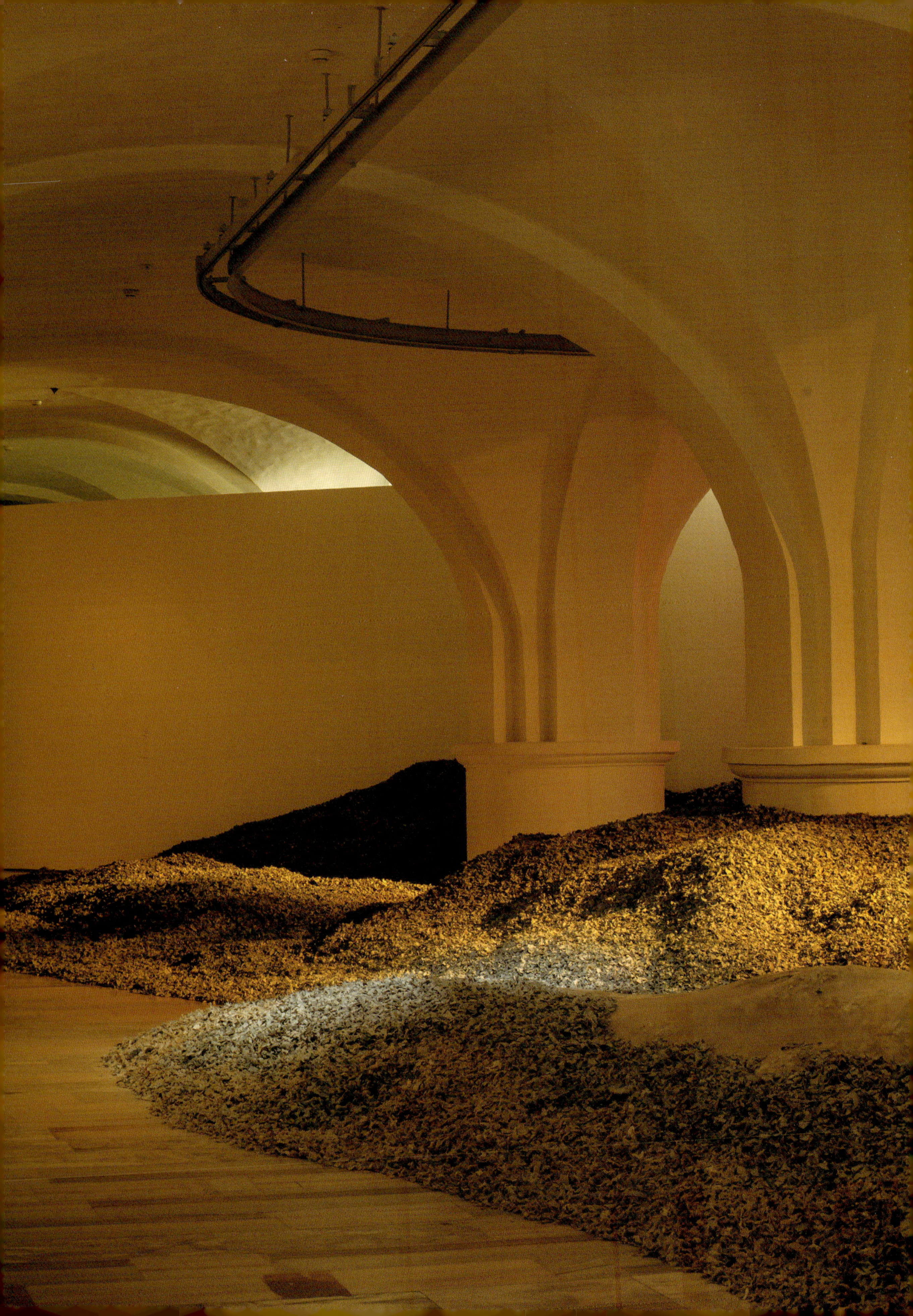

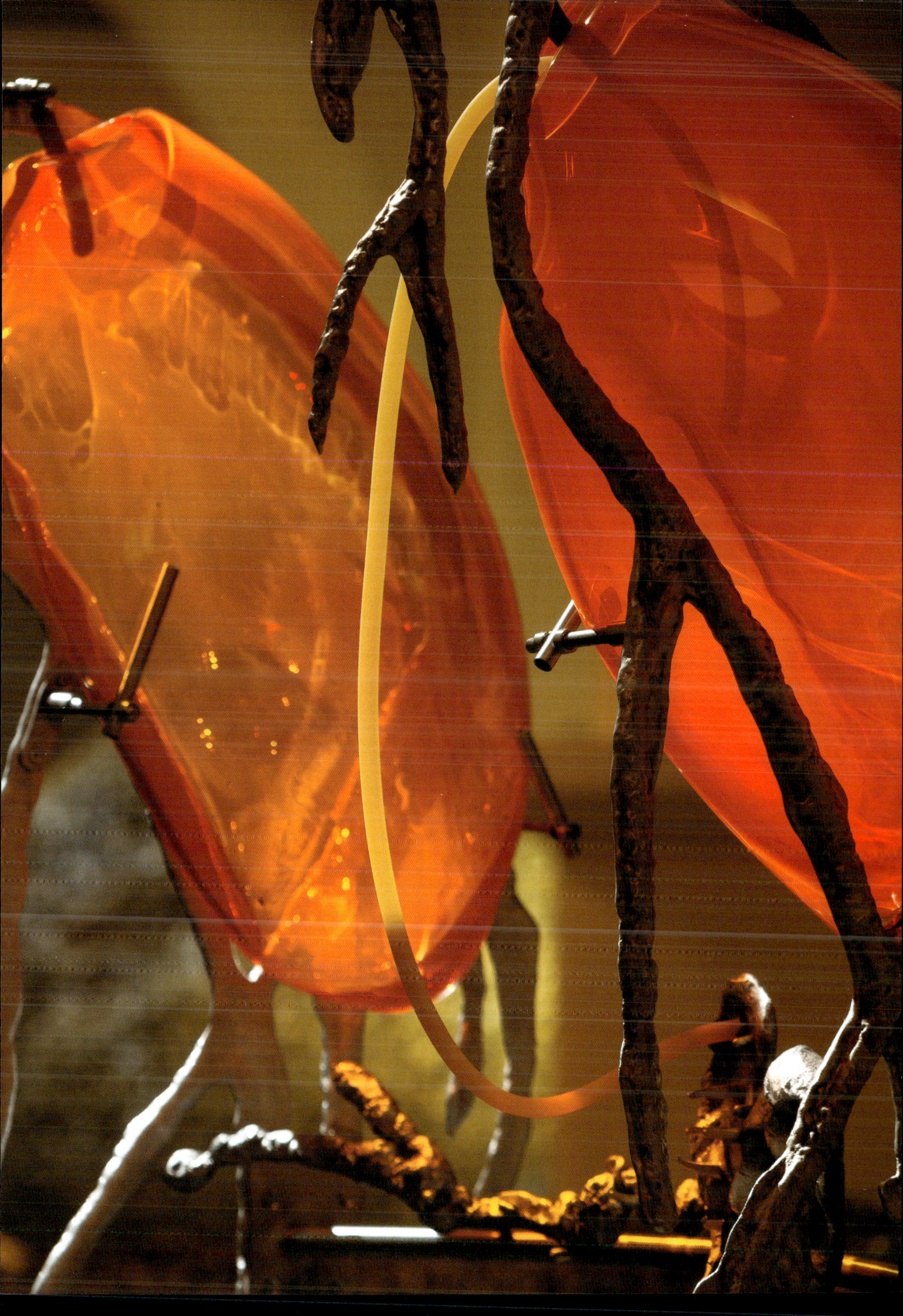

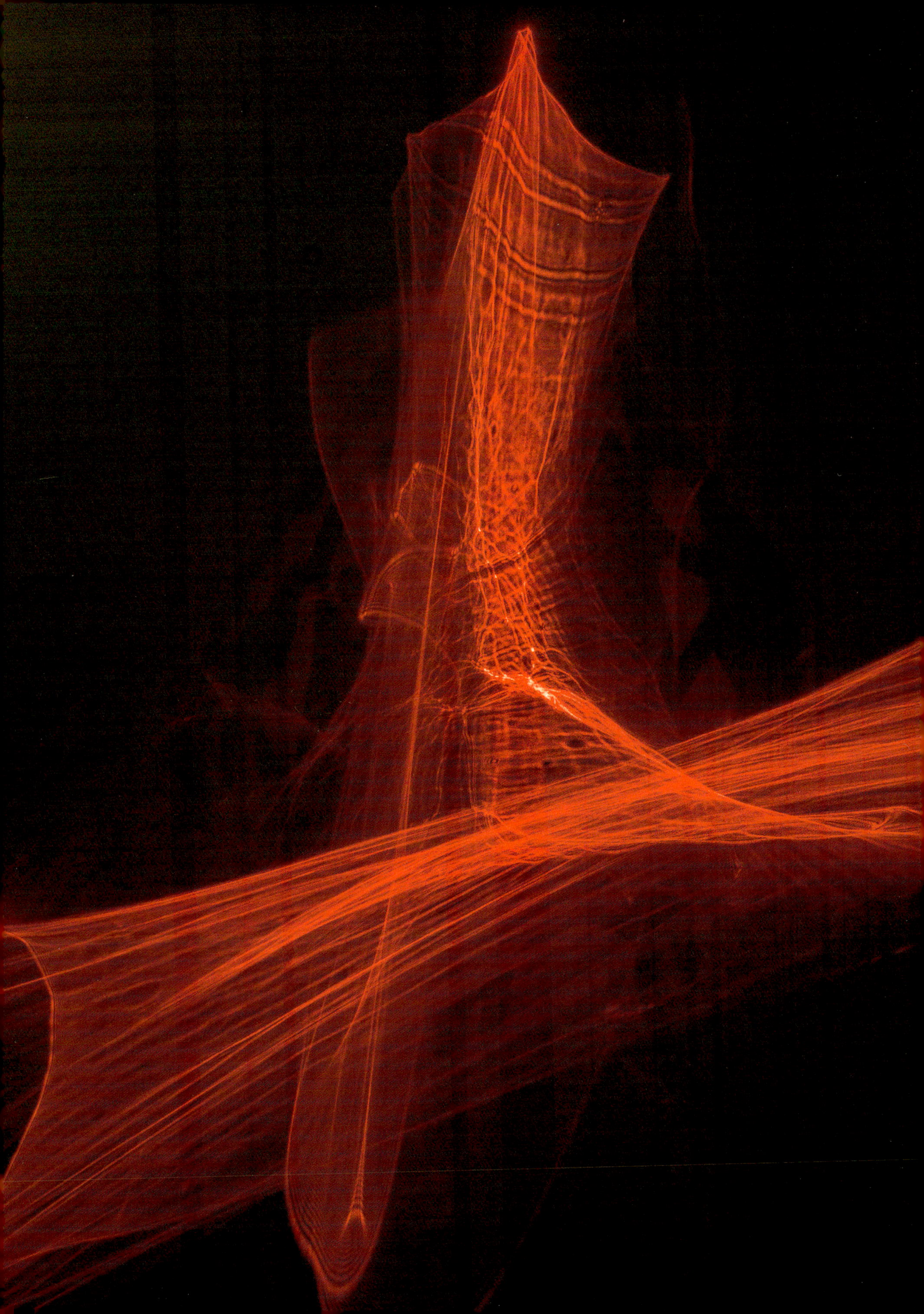

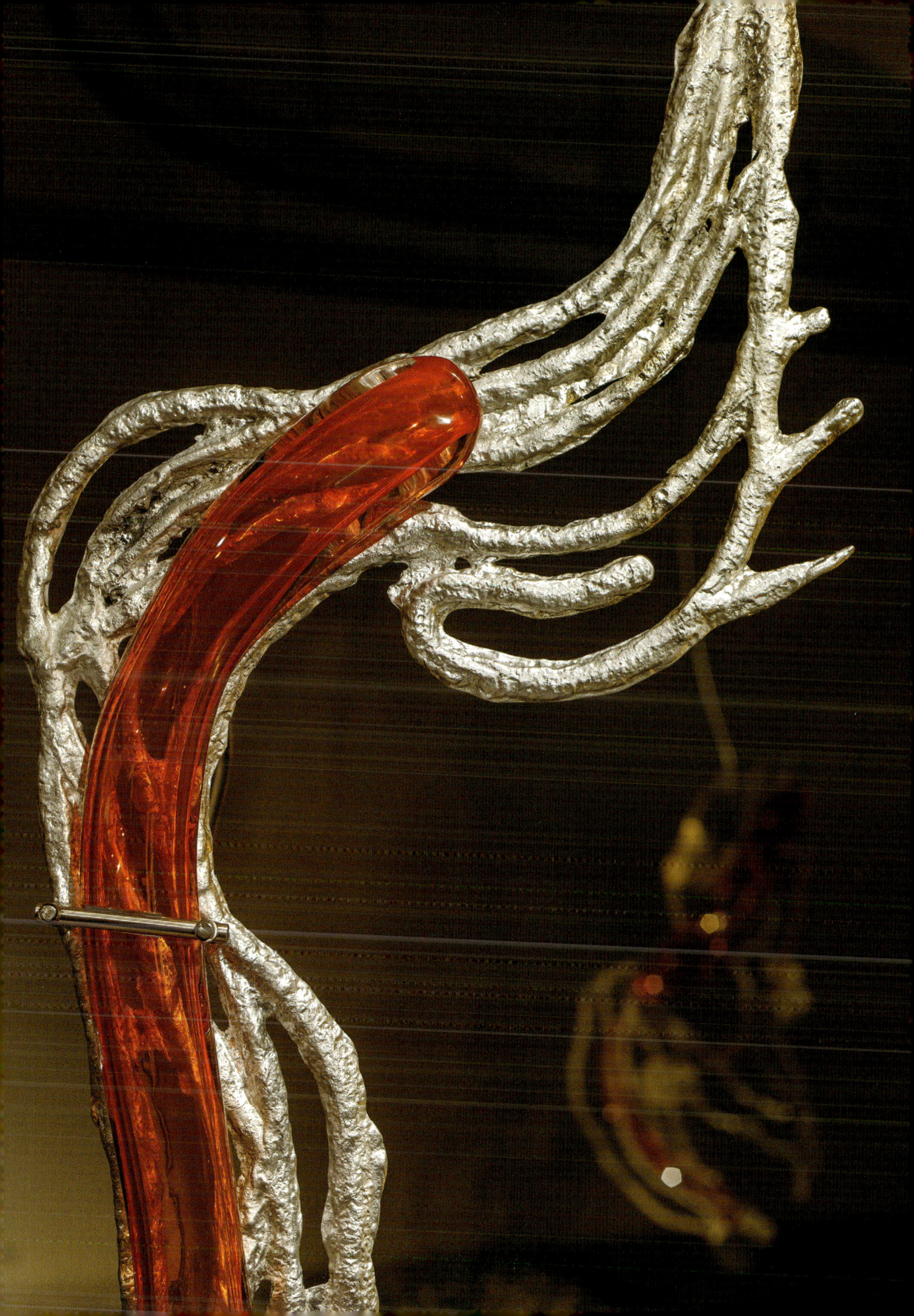

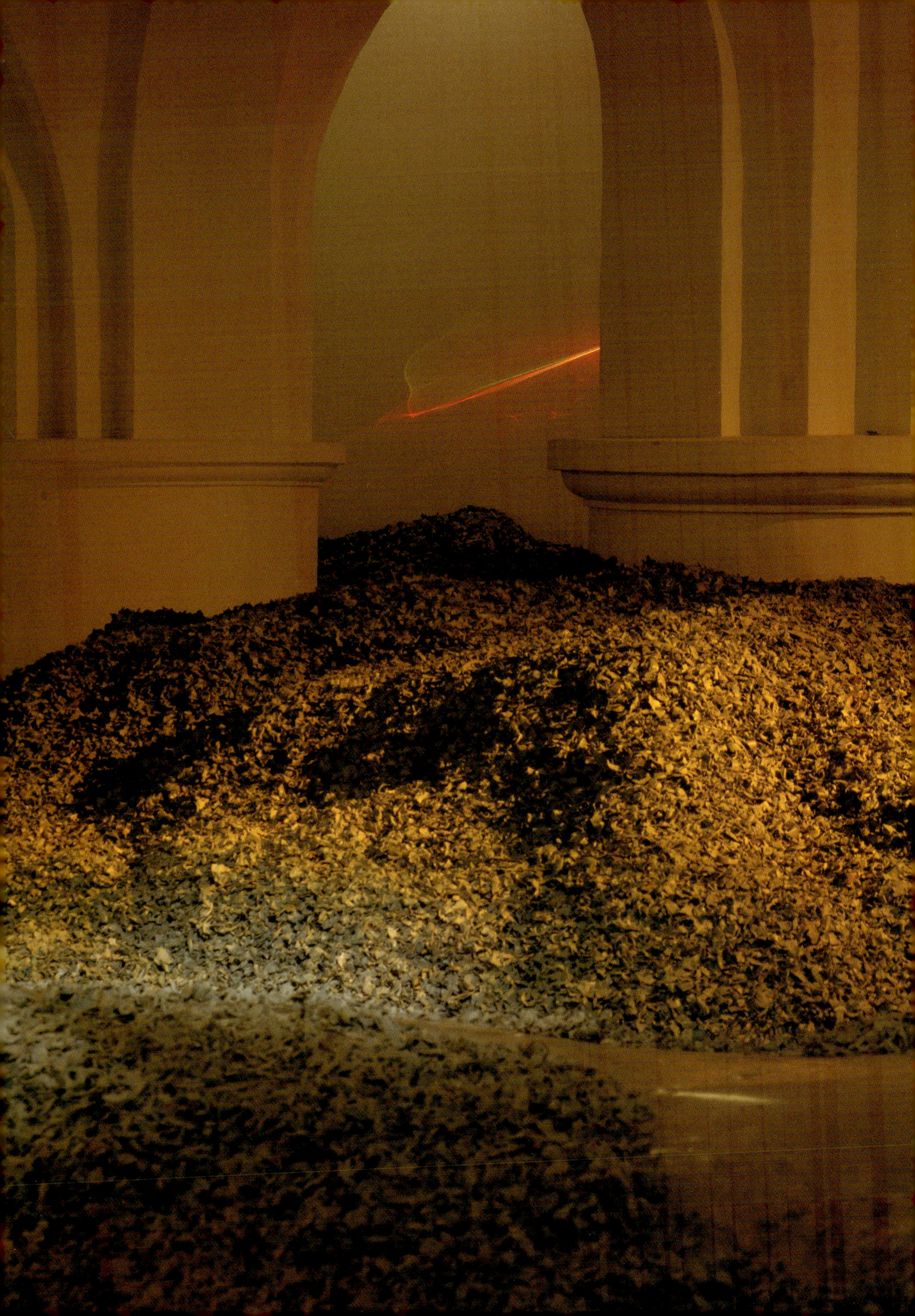

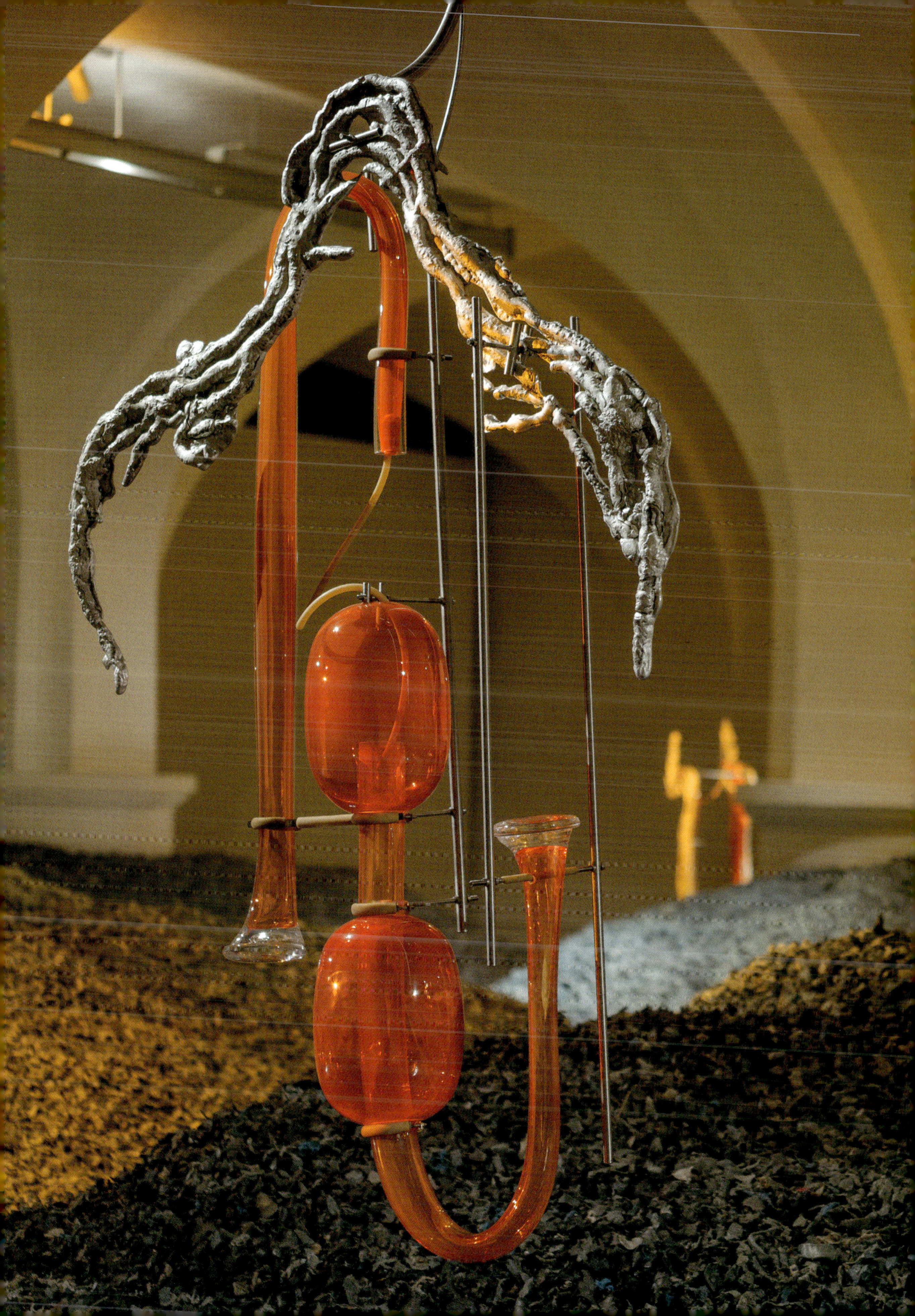

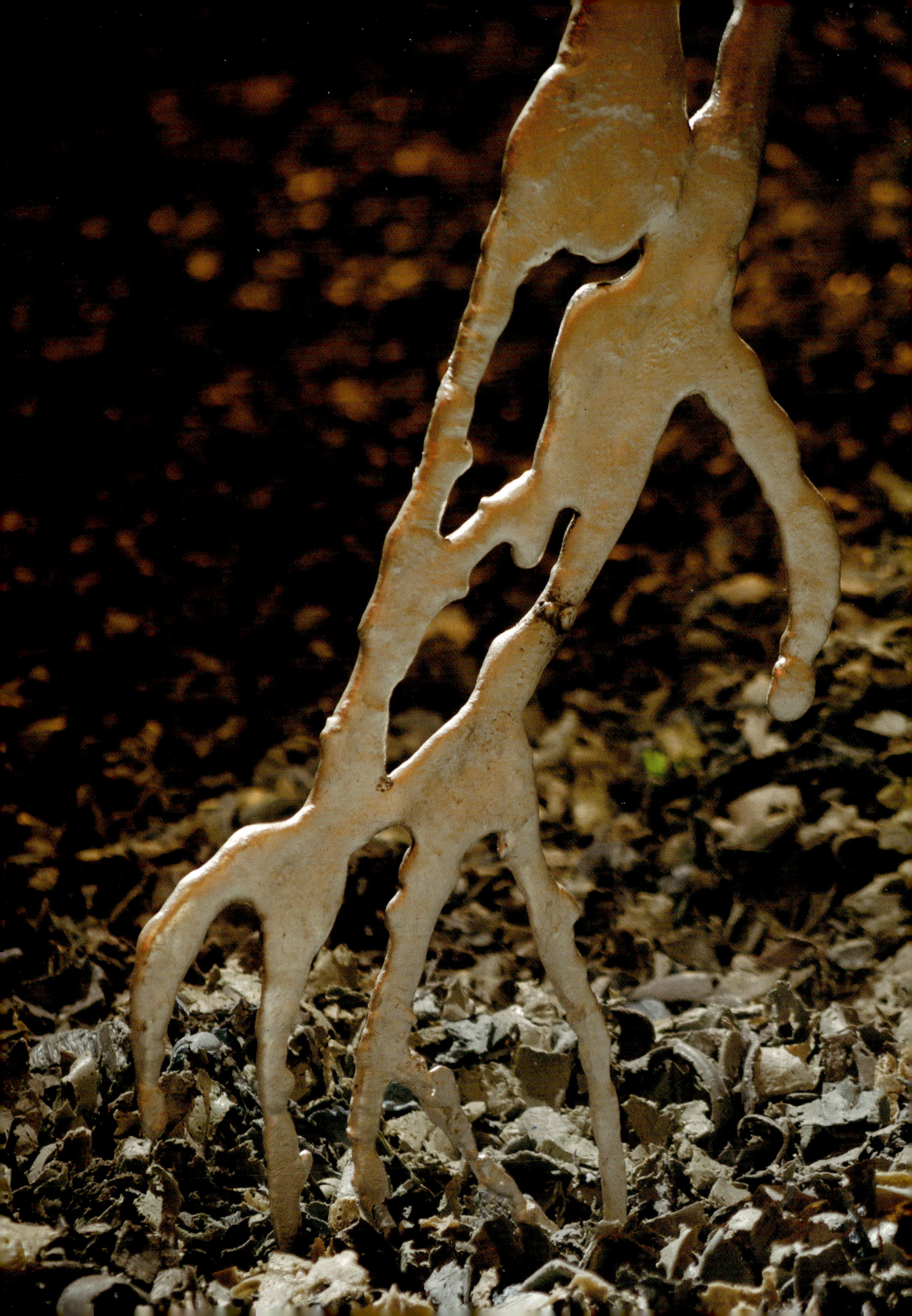

João Laia

Curator of the Lithuanian Pavilion
at the 60th Edition of La Biennale di Venezia

A Planet in Transition: On Pakui Hardware's Inflamed Landscapes

Deep medicine requires new cosmologies, ones that can braid our lives with the planet and the web of life around us. The anatomy of justice stretches from the hospital to the forest, from the ocean to the school, from the prison to the sky. The process of decolonizing must be deeply unsettling and highly creative. It will transform us all.
— Rupa Marya and Raj Patel[1]

We are not simple witnesses of what is occurring. We are the bodies through which the mutation arrives to stay. The question is no longer who we are but what are we going to become.
— Paul B. Preciado[2]

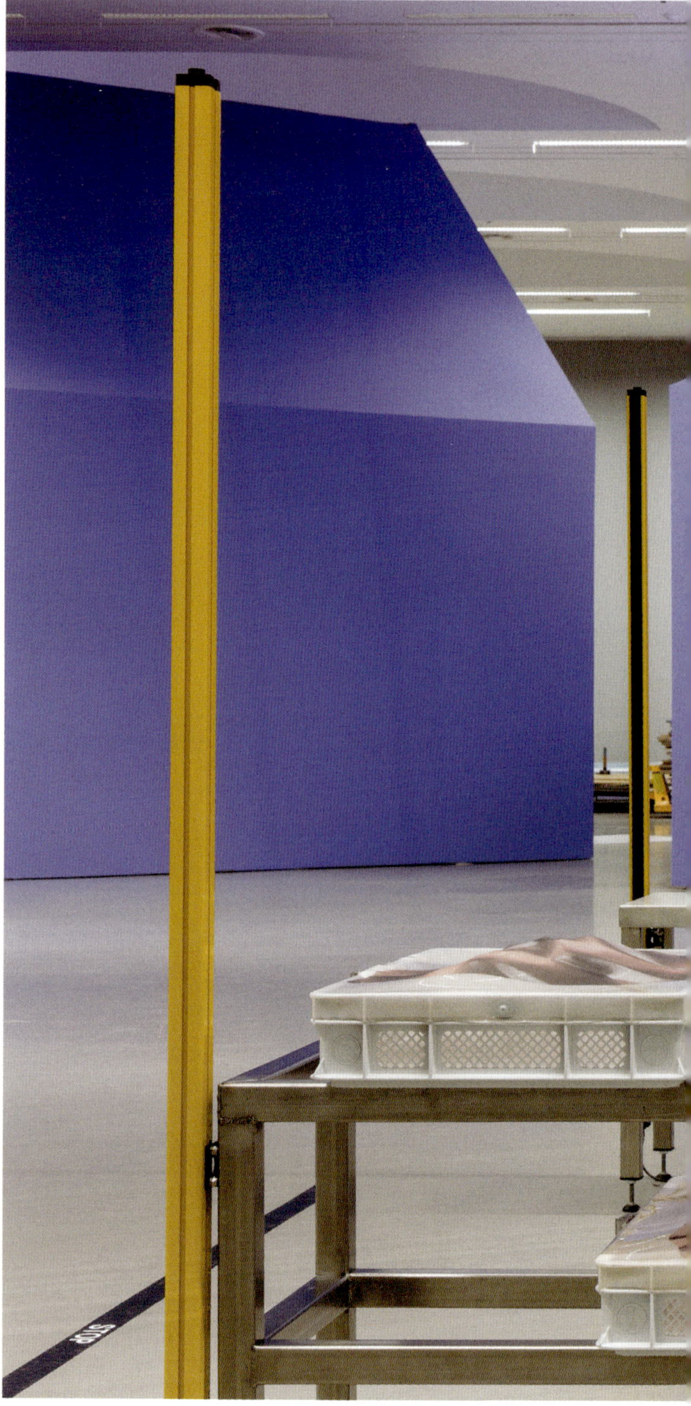

1   Rupa Marya and Raj Patel, *Inflamed: Deep Medicine and the Anatomy of Injustice* (New York: Farrar, Straus and Giroux, 2021), 525.
2   Paul B. Preciado, *Disphoria Mundi* (Barcelona: Editorial Anagrama, 2022), 38.

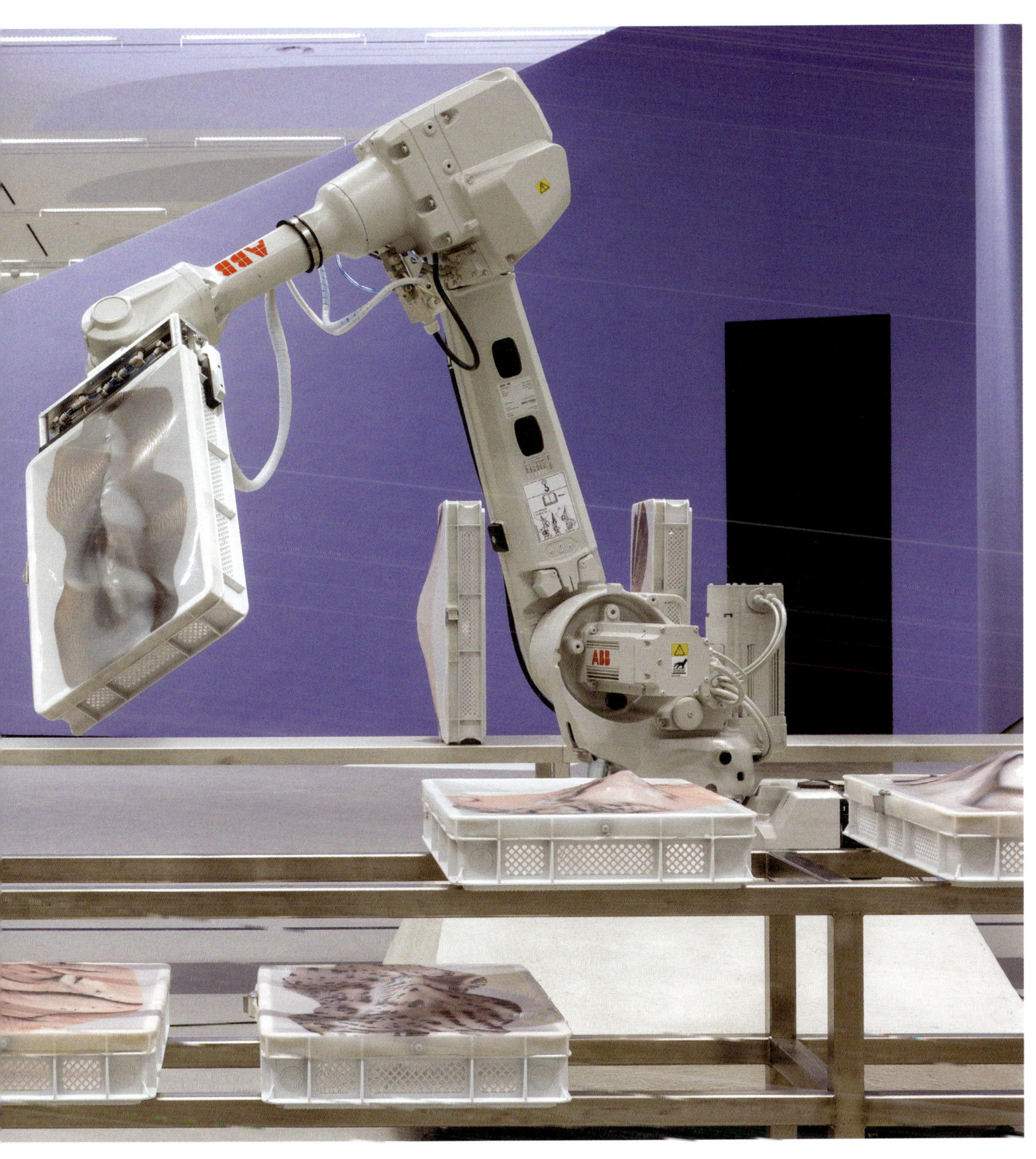

 ↑→ Pakui Hardware, *Hesitant Hand*, 2017. Installation view, National Gallery of Art, Vilnius, 2017
Photo: Andrej Vasilenko. Courtesy the artists and carlier | gebauer, Berlin & Madrid

Deeply grounded in the now, Pakui Hardware's practice regularly focuses on the bodily as a means to look at networks of belonging and their impact on how bodies operate and unfold. Throughout their work, the duo investigates the manners through which living wetware interacts with and is part of mutually defining systems of economy, politics, and technology. This integrated speculative approach imagines strange yet realistic sci-fi universes, guises of the multiple possible present-futures currently taking shape. *Metaphysics of the Runner*, their first project, presented in 2014, analyzed how jogging is embedded in consumption dynamics, impacting one's behavior and self-perception in light of their inscription and participation in contemporary regimes of representation. Health and well-being are consistent fields of interest through which the duo analyze how Michel Foucault's view of medicine as an instrument of control continues to be operative as part of current conceptions of labor and productivity. For the Lithuanian Pavilion of La Biennale di Venezia in 2024, the duo conceives of the planet as an ailing body, enlarging their scope of action by looking at the multiplicity of agencies that form the constitution of the celestial-visceral entity. In so doing, they design an environment that is both a map of our times as well as a cosmological setting acknowledging the multilayered quality of life on Earth. This gesture is augmented through a dialogue with Marija Terese Rožanskaitė (1933–2007), a long-standing reference in the artists' practice, whose inclusion adds a historical layer to the immersive contemporary proposal.

Active starting in the late 1950s, Rožanskaitė became known for canvases depicting bleak scenarios related to medical procedures such as examinations or surgeries, often documenting the relationship between humans and machines. Toward the late 1990s and early 2000s, Rožanskaitė's practice exited the canvas to interact with outdoor landscapes, particularly forests and rivers. This move underlined the artist's interest in the porous entanglement of society and nature, denoting ecological and cosmological concerns, which were already present in a more subtle manner in some of her paintings. Rožanskaitė's work is frequently read as a reaction to the oppressive social context of Eastern European Communist regimes. This perspective gains traction in view of other events documented therein, such as deportations (experienced by the artist and her family in 1941) or resistance against the regime.[3] Sharing positions that react to the elusive, albeit loaded, contours and structures of their corresponding contexts, Rožanskaitė and Pakui Hardware present a number of continuities. For example: Rožanskaitė's engagement with the then-omnipresent Communist state finds a parallel in the duo's analysis of neoliberalism's current ubiquitous agency. In similar ways, both practices subsequently expand to incorporate immersive and holistic methodologies, whereby previous objects of study become part of a multitude of forces combined in larger entities.

Pakui Hardware's work enacts a number of overlapping investigations that offer clear analytical vectors. One such strand employs a method similar to dissecting: isolating elements in order to study their participation in wider networks as well as to identify and analyze the impacts of such contexts on those particular objects. Examples of this procedure are found in projects such as *Hesitant Hand* (2016) or *Virtual Care* (2021), which, echoing Rožanskaitė, investigate the relationship between technology and humans. Whereas *Hesitant Hand* looked into automated robotic choreographies reminiscent of distribution axes such as Amazon fulfillment centers, *Virtual Care* projected a liminal space akin to a clinical surgery. Both scenarios were emptied of humans and hovered between physical materiality and digital virtuality, placing mechanical-digital arms center stage as icons of current abstracted bodily dynamics. In a move already implied in their name, "Pakui," drawing from Hawaiian mythology,[4] the duo also experiments with cosmological prospects. Their employment of mechanical-digital arms and hybrid factory-laboratories are clear instances of this speculative approach, arguably finding heightened examples in the totemic entities of otherness found in *Extrakorporal* (2018) and *Creatures of Habit* (2017). Whereas the latter echoes

3   Laima Kreivytė, *Marija Terese Rožanskaitė: X-Rays* (Vilnius: Lithuanian Art Museum, 2013), 5, 111.
4   The duo's name was coined by curator Alex Ross in 2014: "Pakui Hardware refers to Pakui, the special attendant of a Hawaiian goddess, who could circle the island of Oahu six times a day. Thus, Pakui Hardware is high-speed and brand politics as a mythical semio-commodity, as well as a desire to transcend material limitations." Inga Lāce, "Pakui Hardware on Entanglements between Bodies, Economy and Technological Development," *Echo Gone Wrong*, March 20, 2019, https://echogonewrong.com/pakui-hardware-entanglements-bodies-economy-technological-development/.

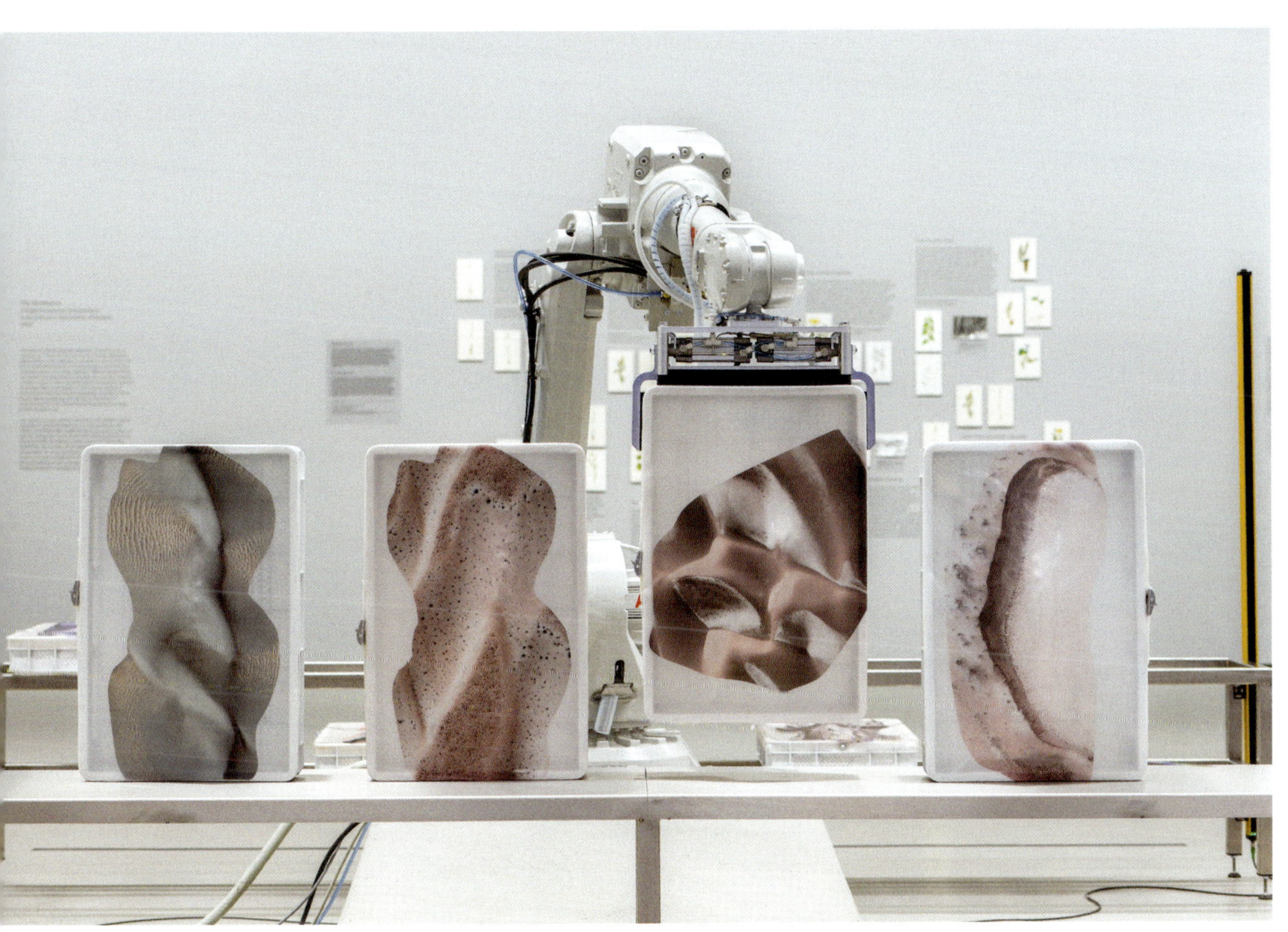

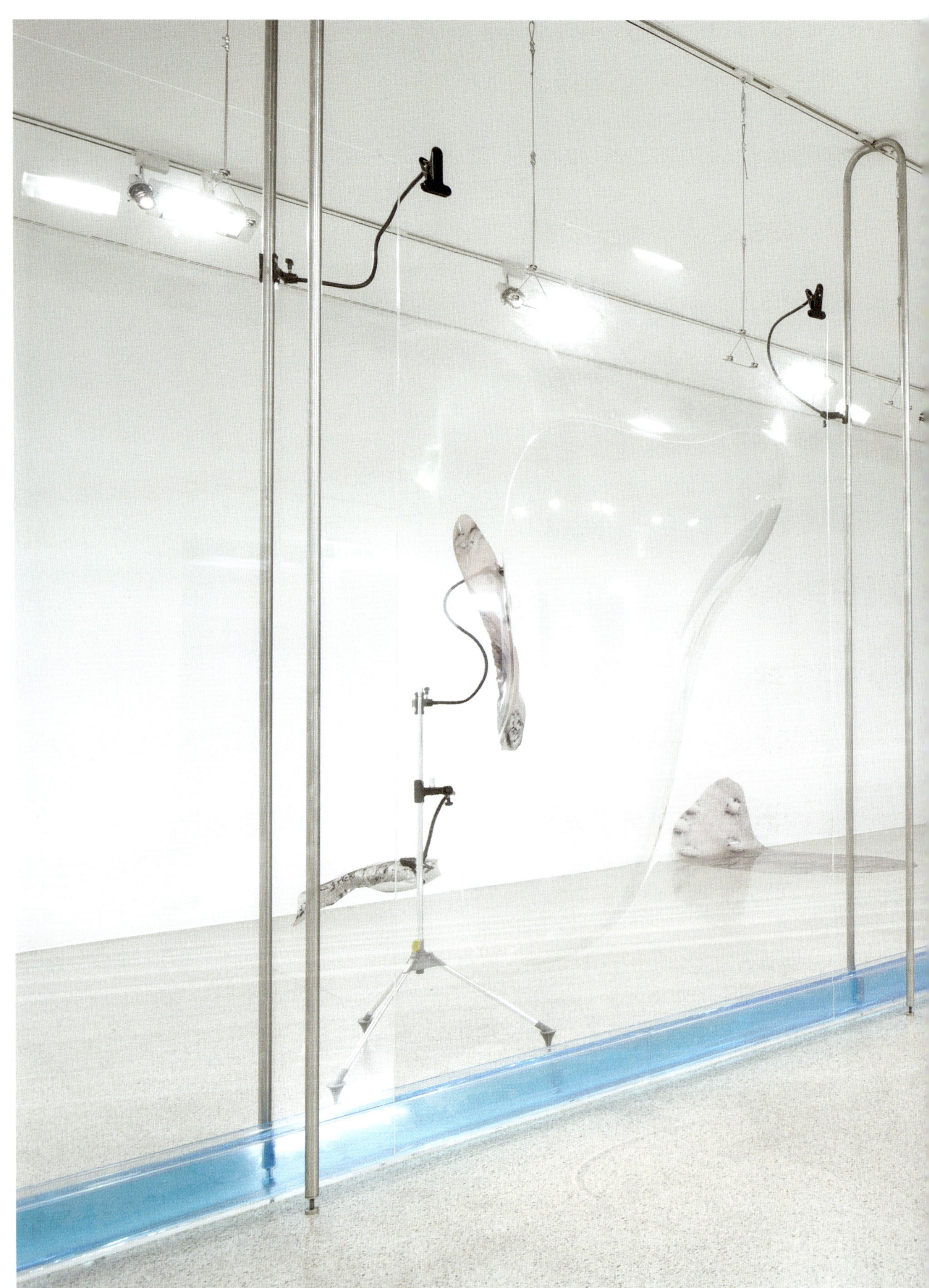

↑→ Pakui Hardware, *Vanilla Eyes*, 2016. Installation view, MUMOK, Vienna, 2016
Photo: Ugnius Gelguda. Courtesy MUMOK, Vienna

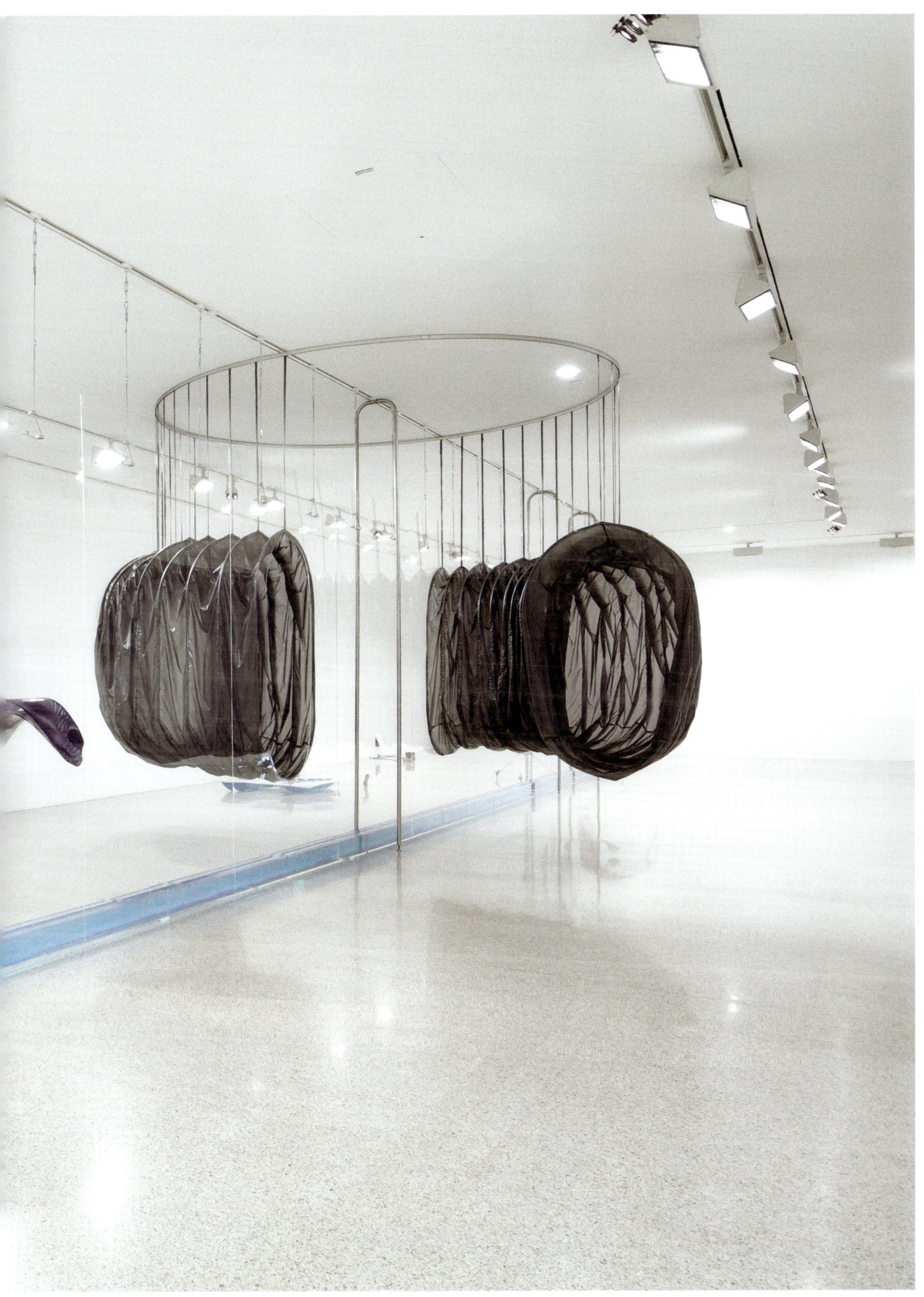

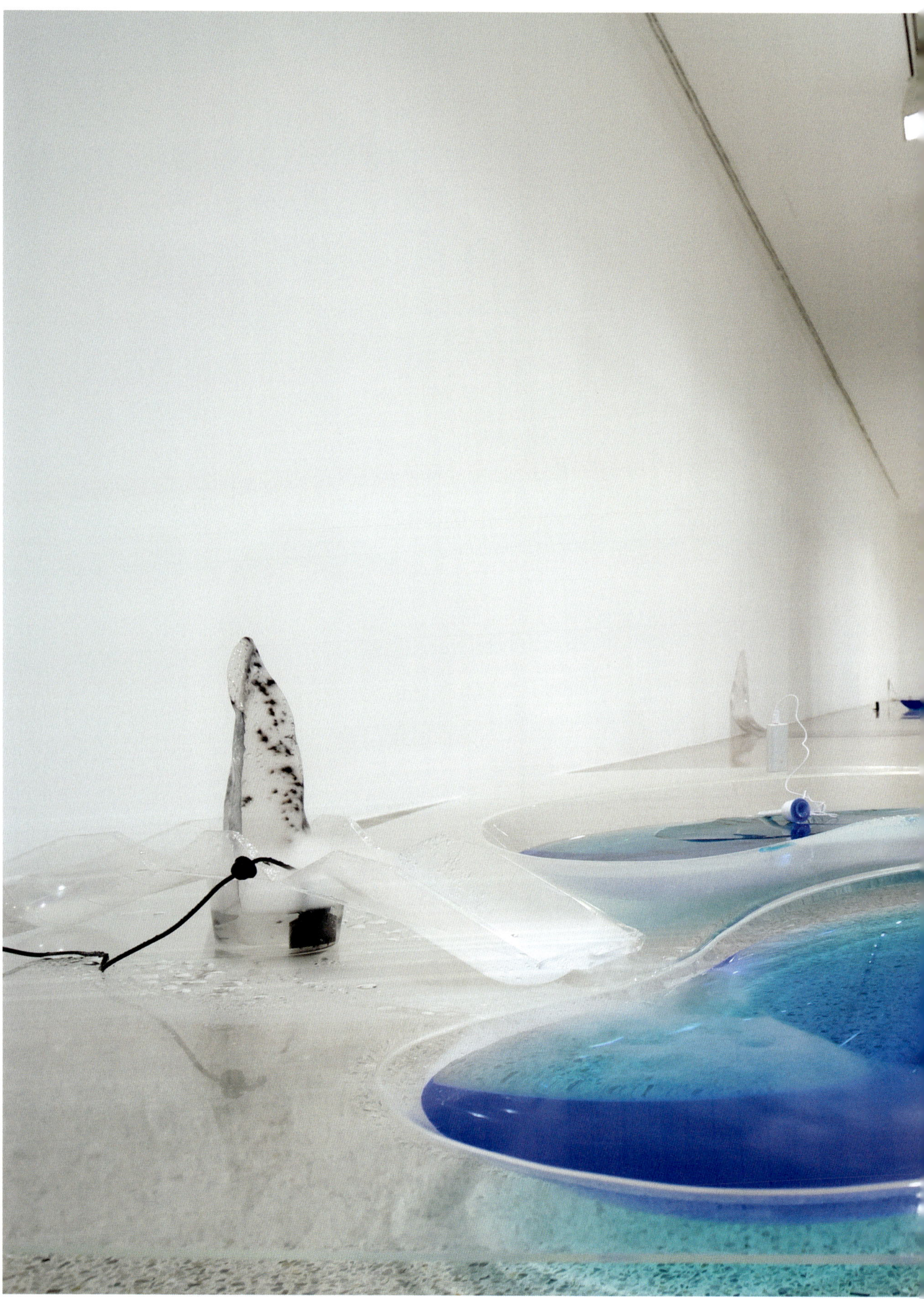

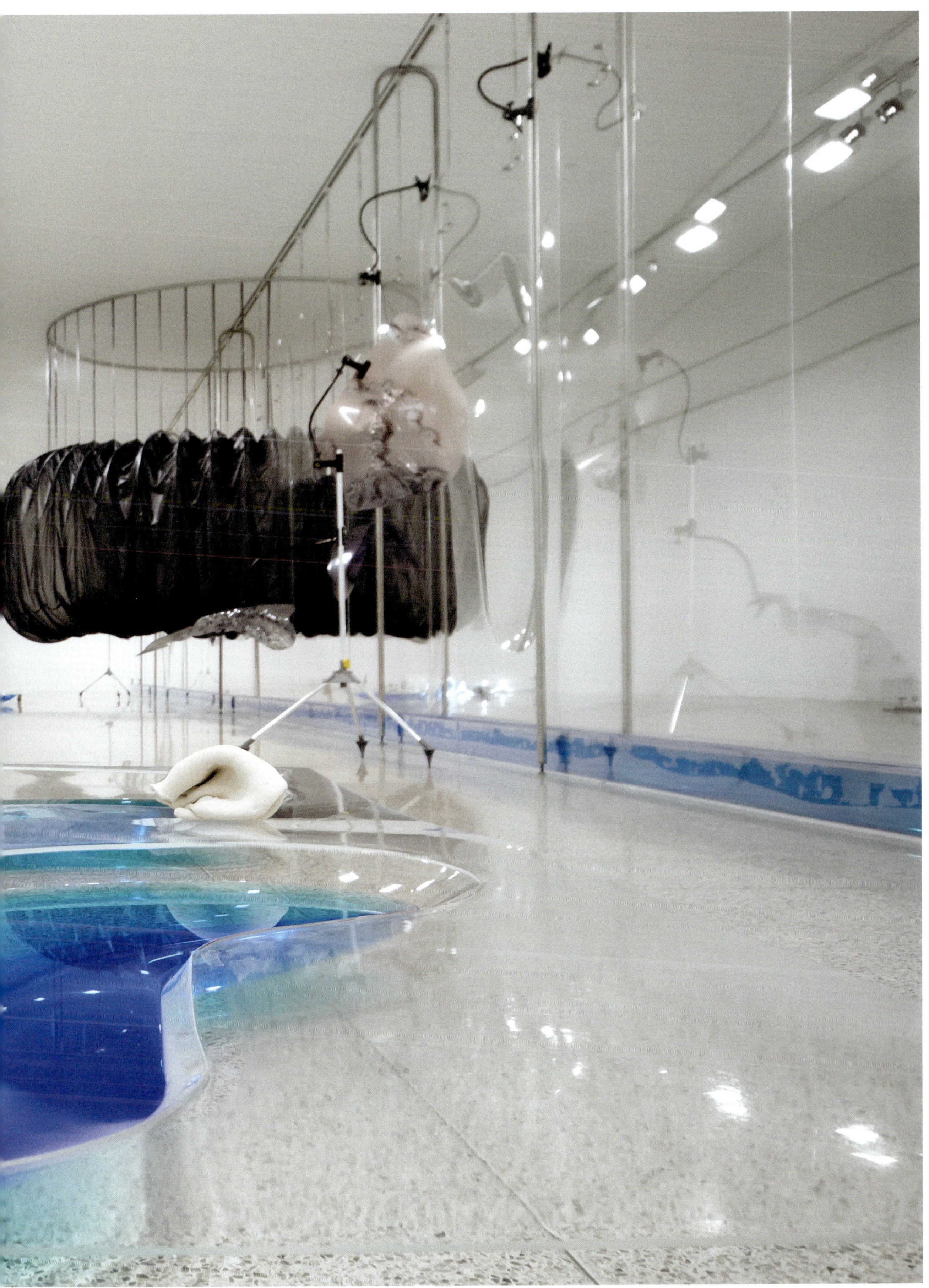

their recurrent interest in automation and a proposed hybrid machine-human species, the former presents a number of bodies half-way between ritualistic masks and shamanistic figures. Both scenarios design synthetic assemblies to experiment with alternative conceptions of the world.

In addition, several cases demonstrate a pronounced interest in materiality, namely in the juxtaposition of elements and textures via the employment of glass, plastic, resin, seeds, and wiring, among others. *The Return of Sweetness* (2018) and *Vanilla Eyes* (2016) are good examples of this line of work, which, like *Hesitant Hand* or *Virtual Care*, echo the guise of a hybrid factory-laboratory and bring to mind an updated form of Rožanskaitė's spatial configurations. *The Return of Sweetness* looks into how the engineering of metabolic relations is shaping reality to produce artificial and yet organic outputs. *Vanilla Eyes* designs a space similar to an incubator of mysterious life forms; because of its immersive features, it is an early example of the approach characterizing their current practice, as seen for example in *Underbelly* (2019), a large-scale entity exhibiting its inner visceral mechanics, fully enveloping visitors and reframing them as tools of invasive medicine. More recently, they also incorporate an alchemical aspect into their practice, working with aluminum alloys to create webs of vessels akin to information and bodily systems (cardiac, nervous, or lymphatic, for example). This approximation to the magic of alchemy strengthens their shaping of a cosmological universe, disrupting straightforward categorizations present in Western scientific thought, which focuses on isolated figures to disregard larger contexts of implication. Through their previous employment of metal and glass, this approach was hinted at in instances such as *Virtual Care* and becomes particularly present in their most recent endeavor.

Presented at the Lithuanian Museum of Art, *Inflammation* (2023) is a large-scale immersive installation in which hybrid aluminum and glass bodies orbit a synthetic landscape. Like the project in Venice to which it served as an introduction, the Vilnius configuration of *Inflammation* drew from the work of Rupa Marya and Raj Patel. In their 2021 book *Inflamed: Deep Medicine and the Anatomy of Injustice*, Marya and Patel map how present-day social, political, economic, and ecological issues that read as inflammations (the reaction of living tissue to injury or infection) are grounded in histories of colonial exploitation and extraction. The authors argue that the path to healing may be found by addressing long-standing inequalities, among humans but also between humans and other-than-human agents. To care for the planet-as-body, one must abandon an individualist conception of life and move toward an intricate web of mutually dependent beings, achieving a state of balance named as homeostasis.[5] Accordingly, Pakui Hardware constantly question "clear-cut" distinctions such as artificial and natural, synthetic and organic, physical and virtual, or self and other. The liminal situations they create are a means of addressing the critical moment we inhabit, and devising other ways of imagining life that manifest as stories of other possible worlds. In *Inflammation* they continue in this line, materializing bodies that are at once familiar and foreign, connecting with an enlarged web of relations and replacing singularity with collectivity.

Inflammation reacts against the tipping point we are inhabiting, when crisis feels overwhelming, overarching, and permanent. The secular Western divide between society and nature, leading to understanding humans as resources (in the capitalist sense) and all other entities as means of production, has not only dehumanized ourselves but also led to exploitative relationships with other-than-humans, breaking the magical homeostatic "animacy of life itself."[6] The current critical situation affecting fields such as ecology, economics, politics, and technology manifests for example in ever-more-frequent extreme weather events, financial crashes, the return of exclusionary nativist positions, and the rise of algorithmic surveillance technologies. In the words of Marya and Patel: "The modern world in all its structures is out of balance, leading to bodies that are badly damaged by chronic inflammation."[7] In the midst of such, feelings of anxiety and impotence emerge, further

5   Marya and Patel, *Inflamed*, 138.
6   Marya and Patel, *Inflamed*, 39.
7   Marya and Patel, *Inflamed*, 405.

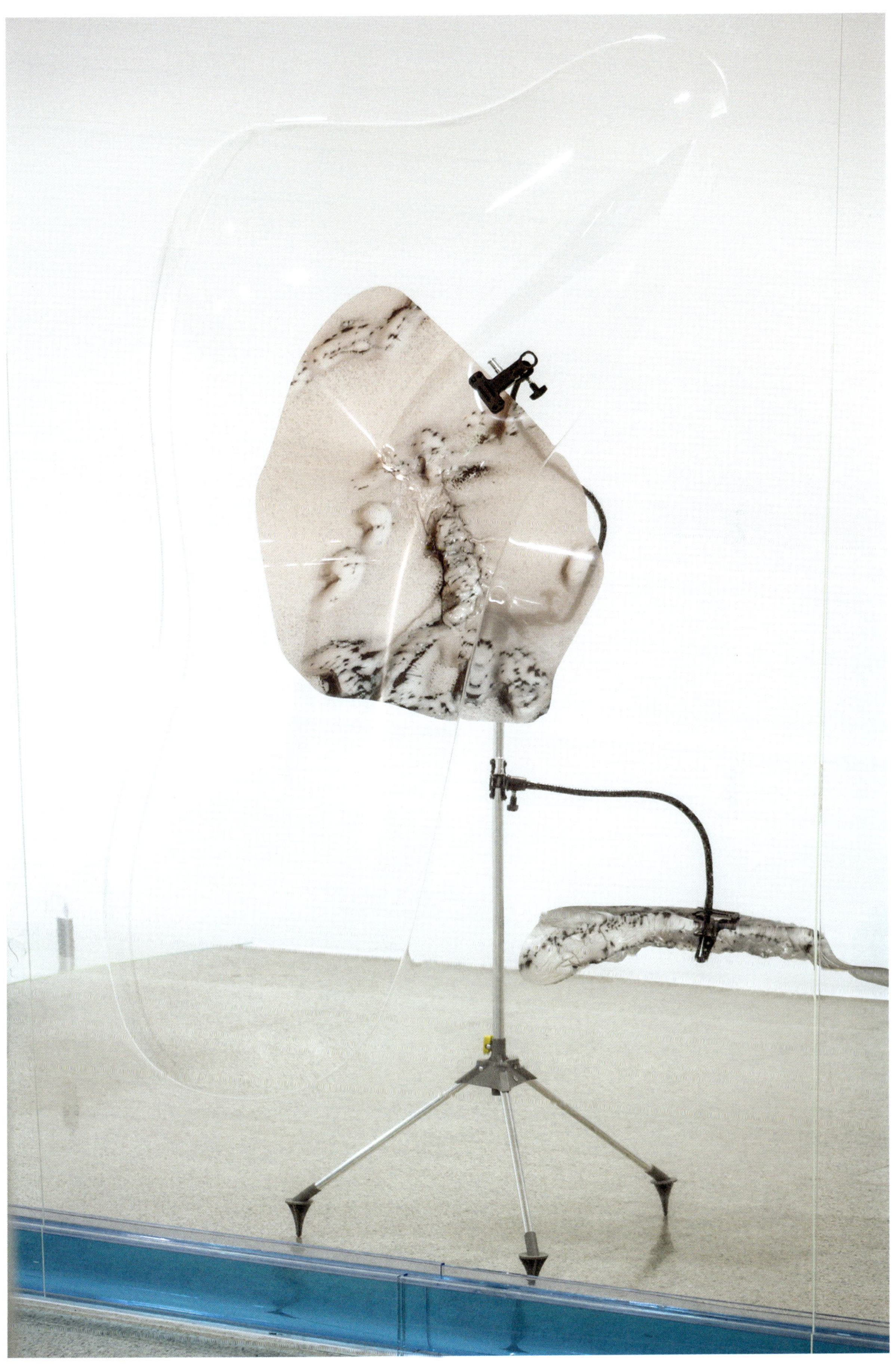

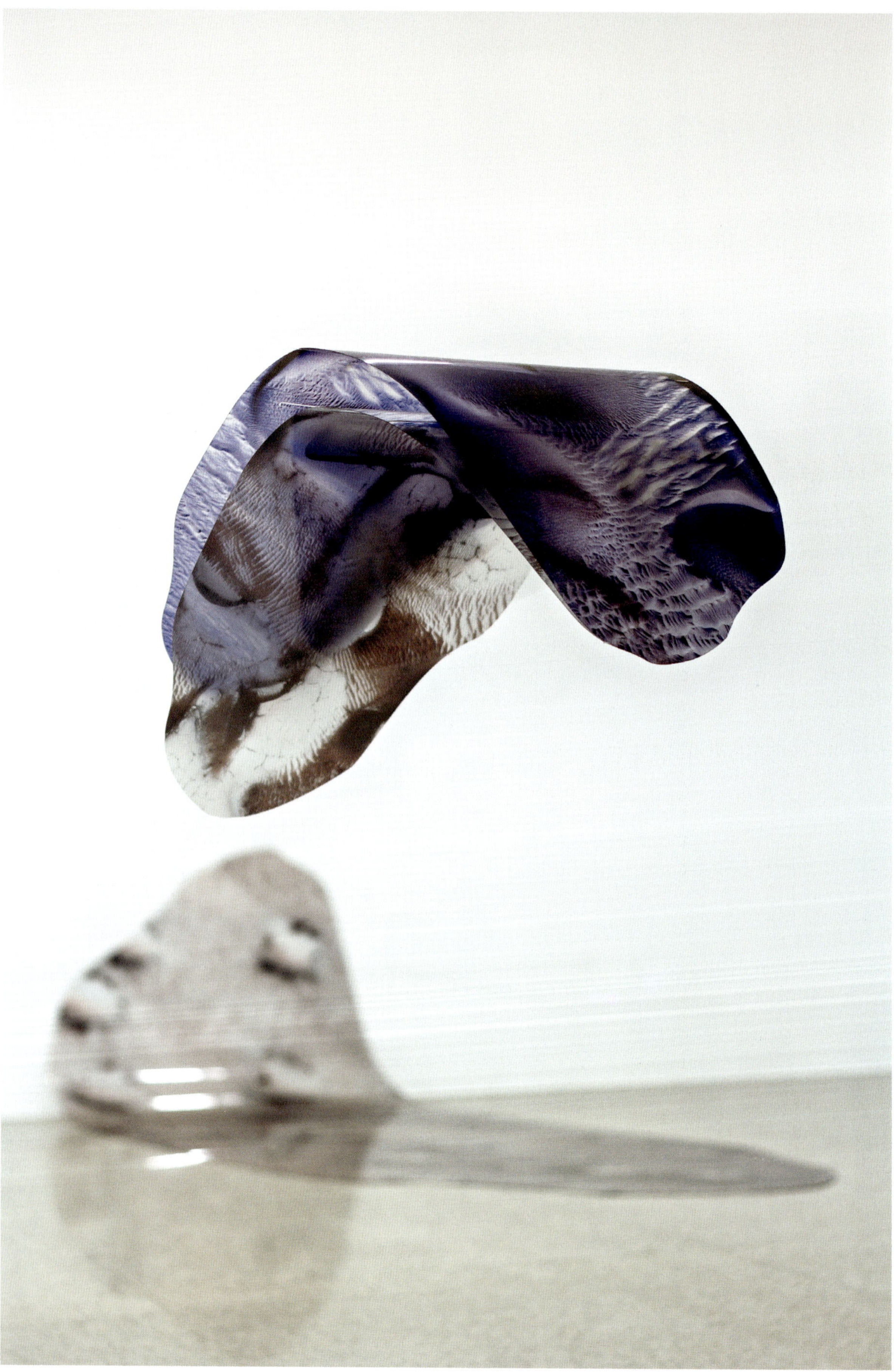

symptoms of our inflamed condition. It feels difficult to imagine a way out of such a burning locus, particularly when dominant narratives of fragmentation preempt the potential of communal efforts. In the words of philosopher Paul B. Preciado: "We don't see nor do we understand the world, we perceive it by wrecking it through the narrow categories that inhabit us. The pain we often feel while alive is the pain of this denial of the world and its sense."[8] Preciado refers to the current moment of crisis as "dysphoria mundi," which is not a personal condition but rather a planetary one.

Inflammation's intense ambience echoes the critical moment we inhabit; its mechanical glass and metal bodies circling a dead scenery reflect the extreme processes encircling all life forms on the planet. It also offers additional layers, staging a challenging and seductive setting to reconnect with otherness. Pakui Hardware's interest in materiality offers a number of possibilities to revamp current nihilistic positions. By radiating as antennae, roots, or veins, the aluminum elements suggest rare earth materials matching the stratification of history and how history "becomes embodied, written inside our cells, carried in our molecules," deposited inside all beings.[9] At the same time, whereas in other projects glass signaled the liquid features of our sped-up, morphing present, here it also becomes a tool "to create a visual connection" obliterating a "sense of boundary between inside and outside."[10] Investigating the history of glass, Matthew Ziff reminds us how the material creates a transparency that allows for exploration and a sense of connectivity. For Ziff, glass enables one "to see out into the surrounding world . . . to identify where you are, to be able to form a worldview that includes self reference." Through glass we are "in relations to elements that are potentially important to you in achieving and maintaining a sense of continuity and of meaning." The author concludes, "The experiential complexities offered in glass environments are at once architectural, psychological, cultural, and economic, and they exist in a revealed, open to inspection state."[11]

Following from their use of materials and in association with the past reflections of Rožanskaitė, *Inflammation* materializes a rupture from the promises of past and present techno-utopian narratives to grasp head-on the pressing moment we inhabit, staging a space to reconnect with the unknown and the forgotten. This is a gesture of utmost importance in order to abandon ongoing regimes of extinction. As signaled by Marya and Patel, we need a break from "supremacist cosmologies and institutions . . . prioritizing individuals over communities."[12] In this sense, such an inflamed, dysphoric state can be read not as a generalized collapse, but alternatively as constituting a healing reaction to illnesses. Rather than a monument to our current demise, the eeriness of the installation manifests the current moment of transition, where past forms are collapsing and new ones are taking shape. In the words of Preciado, "It is necessary to understand dysphoria mundi as the effect of a gap, a failure, between two epistemological regimes. Between the petrosexorracial regime inherited from Western modernity and a new regime."[13]

With *Inflammation*, Pakui Hardware offers a manifestation of such a gap, materializing the demise of past positions to animate the emergence of future agencies. We humans, other life forms, and all entities thought of as inanimate on the planet are, in the words of Preciado, "the bodies through which the mutation arrives to stay."[14] *Inflammation* as an inflamed dysphoric landscape becomes an apt reaction to "a state of becoming," holding "many possible futures"[15] that reconnect with the other, offering a space for the unknown where new stories and cosmologies can emerge.

8   Preciado, *Disphoria Mundi*, 19.
9   Marya and Patel, *Inflamed*, 108.
10 Matthew Ziff, "The Role of Glass in Interior Architecture: Aesthetics, Community, and Privacy," *Journal of Aesthetic Education* 38, no. 4 (Winter 2004): 14, 16.
11 Ziff, "The Role of Glass in Interior Architecture," 15, 21.
12 Marya and Patel, *Inflamed*, 447.
13 Preciado, *Disphoria Mundi*, 27.
14 Preciado, *Disphoria Mundi*, 38.
15 Marya and Raj Patel, *Inflamed*, 509.

Petras Išora, Ona Lozuraitytė

Exhibition Environment and Landscape
Architects of the Lithuanian Pavilion
at the 60th Edition of La Biennale di Venezia

Stratigraphy of the Environment

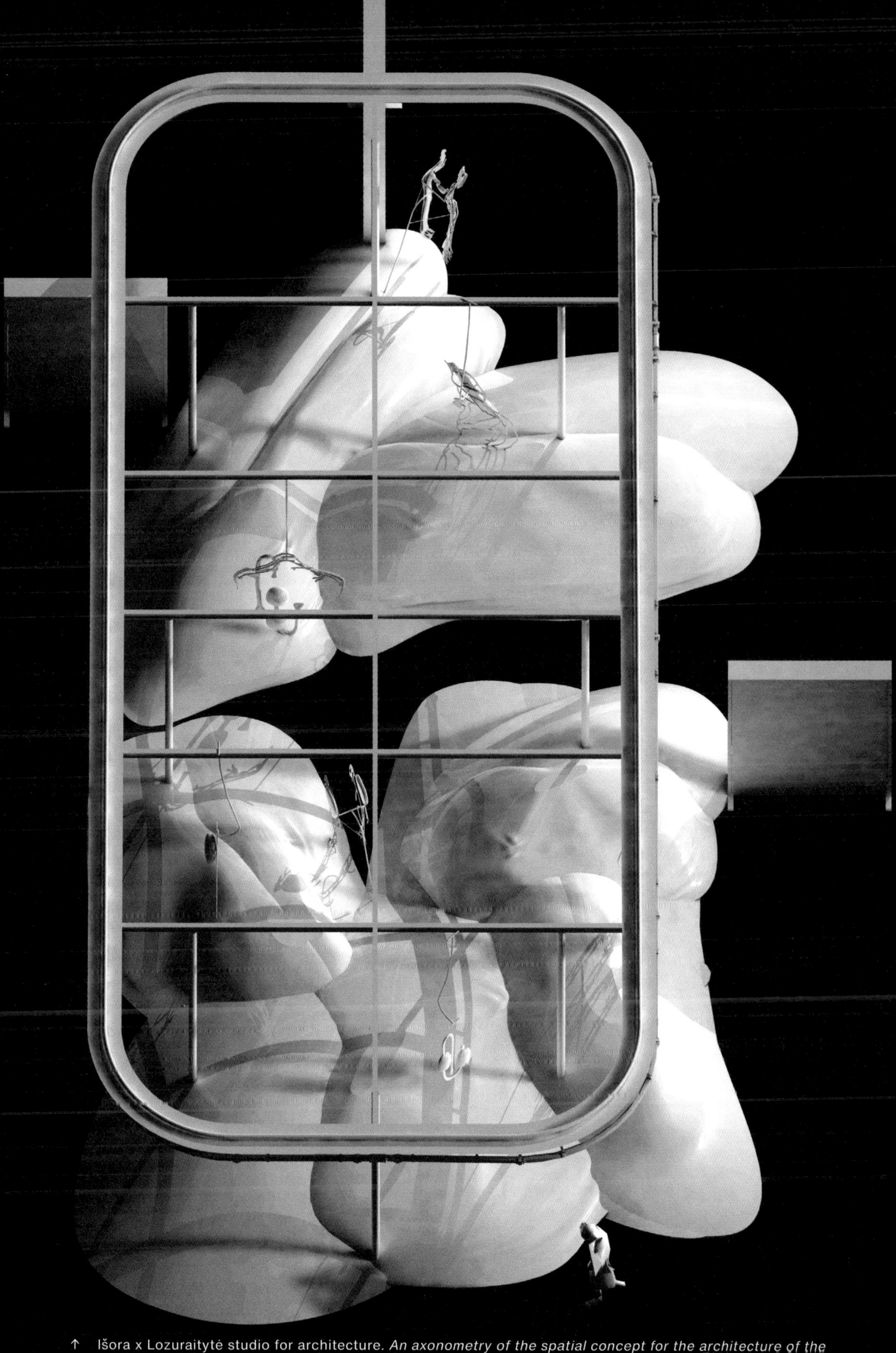

↑ Išora x Lozuraitytė studio for architecture. *An axonometry of the spatial concept for the architecture of the environment for the installation "Inflammation" at the Lithuanian National Pavilion of La Biennale di Venezia, 2024* Courtesy the authors

Estelle Hoy

Imposter Syndrome:

Pavilions Built on Faults de la Terre

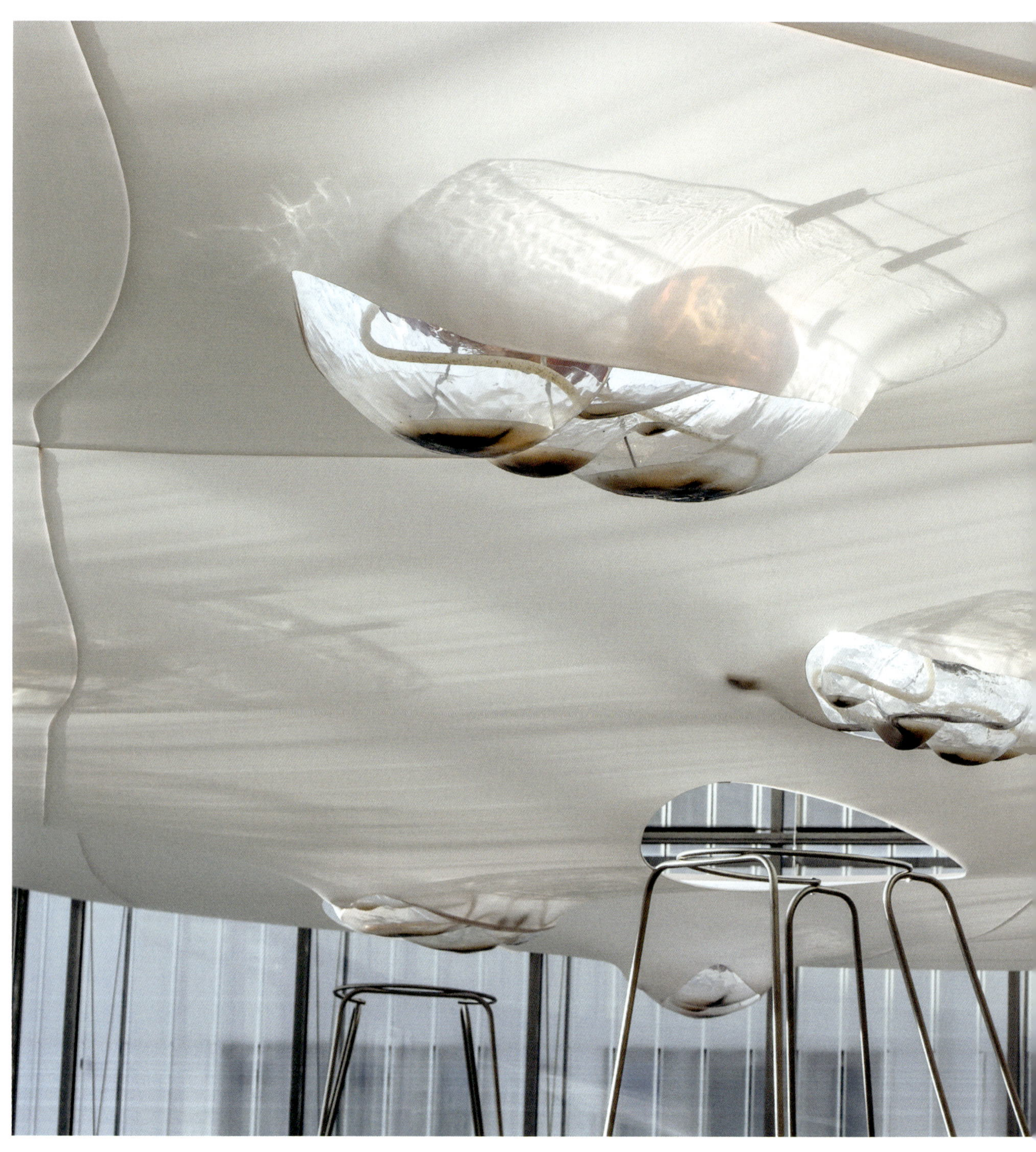

↑→ Pakui Hardware, *Underbelly*, 2019. Installation view, Museum der Bildenden Künste Leipzig, Germany, 2019
Photo: Ugnius Gelguda. Courtesy the artists and carlier | gebauer, Berlin & Madrid

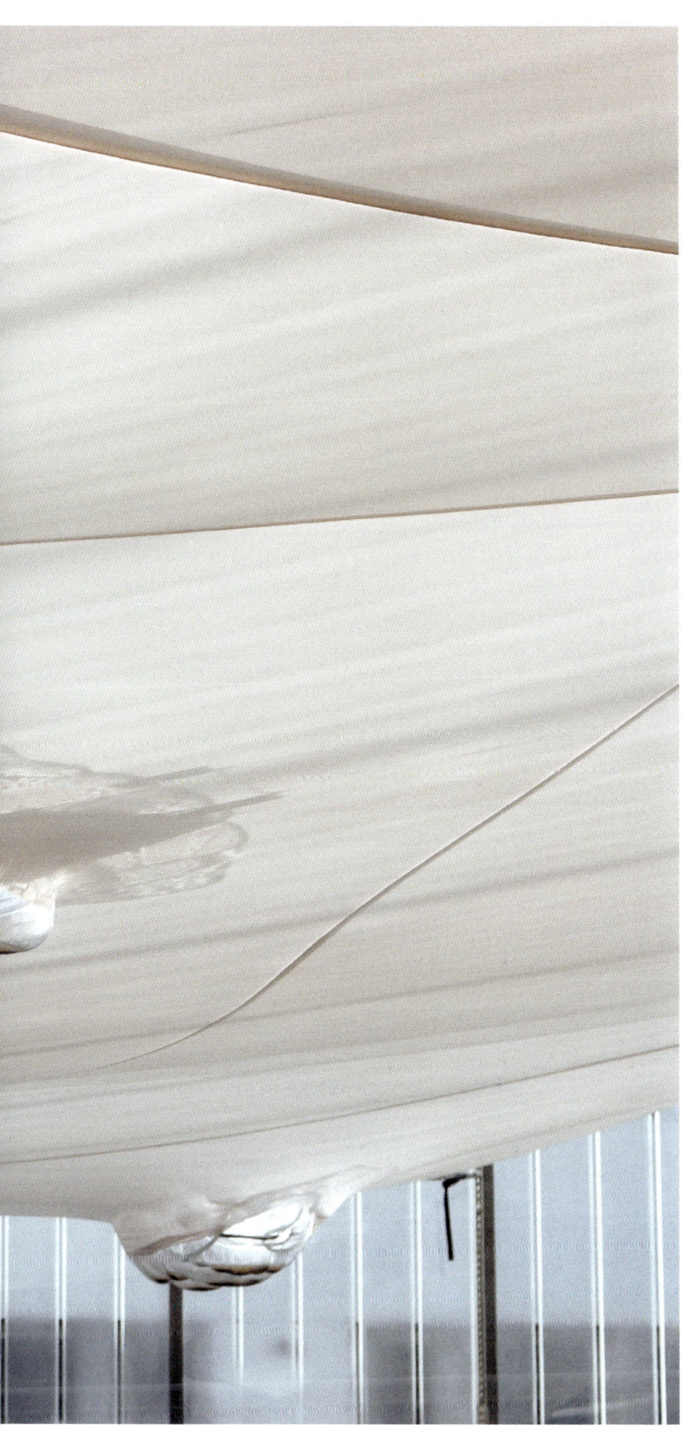

A wound with blood and pus, or the sickly, acrid smell of sweat, of decay, does not
signify death. In the presence of signified
death—a flat encephalograph, for instance—
I would understand, react, or accept. No, as
in true theater, without makeup or masks,
refuse and corpses *show me* what I permanently thrust aside in order to live. These
body fluids, this defilement, this shit are
what life withstands, hardly and with difficulty, on the part of death. There, I am at
the border of my condition as a living being.
—Julia Kristeva, *Powers of Horror:
An Essay on Abjection*, 1980

Scripting the human and porous traces of a modifying future is a dietic intervention Pakui Hardware backs like a surgeon, showing up, mind sterilized, taking up plenty of operating room in the Lithuanian Pavilion at the 60th Venice Biennale with their kinetic, phenotypic socio-artistic changes. Their cup runneth over. The keloid scars and exquisite impressions of our political history are a movable feast. We risk exposure day by day, hour by hour, taking supplements against the irrefutability of time. Attempting to live without attachment to the past, its bio-myths, and its inexorable etiology that floods tenuous human flesh and minds is quiet stupidity. It rejects the notion of a commonplace reality: they're not good genes, they're not bad genes, but by God, they're genes. What does this reveal about ourselves as moving notations of permeability? How to harness self-narrations and inject them into a molecule body perpetually inflamed and in flux, stamped by intimate memories of childhoods and social conditions as complicated as the capricious hormonal wake we embody?

The foreboding prosthetics of Pakui Hardware's artworks and all their inseminating potentialities reveal *aesthetic neuroplasticity*, envisioning myths and mutations that are—incredibly—already under way in our social brains. The artistic duo appreciates the possibilities that the present state of our myelin can afford us and the general intellect this brings about. Since the final years of the last century, and also always, dissonance symptoms and tender rhythms have multiplied in aesthetic sensibility. We now know that the body is equipped with excessively high levels of dutiful plasticity, so we can be recumbent and appropriately wonder: Will the cerebellum and its faux roadblocks succeed in finding a way out of this political labyrinth? Can neural and inflammatory impostors discover new possible conjunctions between the world and the body? Pollinating this aesthetic choreography at the scalar register of the cellular, growing forms like cathected spines, breathing swollen chia seeds, and pink-sieved earth, fragile and quivering above unforgiving fault lines, are Pakui Hardware, whose answer is an indefatigable yes. For the Lithuanian Pavilion

at the Venice Biennale, the artists focus on reframing the relations between the rhythms of the body, the rhythm of the transmitter, and the chaotic, supposedly unyielding universe, sending signs that are no longer filtered by the grids of staid semiotic order. You see, neuroplasticity was once a myth, only accepted by the scientific community in the 1960s. The idea is that neural pathways could change, grow, reorganize, and rewire themselves to function in ways they previously hadn't; a scientific reality, once parable or folklore, becomes a hopeful utopian reality. This serves as a reminder for Pakui Hardware: that which is myth, unattainable, heresy, unfathomable, ridiculous, impossible, fantasy, wishful thinking, or itching delusion can become a splendid material reality.

It's an unpredictable mess with one constant: it is activity dependent.

Paying attention to shy shifts of wind, infections, and the activity of aesthetics, the duo have drip-fed their audience since 2014 with singular, otherworldly installations in hybrid materials collected from Mars or Jupiter: blistered glass, steel, cable, latex rubber, searing aluminum, thermoformed plastic, shredded soil, ladders, seafoam, alien membranes. Phantasmagoric cities are built around collapsing myelin and myths, sighing, humming, and swaying into new, extraterrestrial landscapes of infinitude that are impossible. Or at least thought to be. Their practice is constantly evolving, with material labor rerouting our poriferous existence. This is far from equilibrium. It's important here to consider material adaptation in this way as a complex, dynamic disorder of neural behavior and (ir)regulation, forcing activity in spaces and areas once defunct. They exert exquisite control of what level of cognitive and aesthetic labor goes into making worlds possible, solidifying through action, eschewing the nastiness of planets, and stinging air that will not and cannot serve us. *Utopia is not a myth!* scream Pakui Hardware. Irrigating biological forms have dominated their practice for several years, peering under and through nebulous organs, silicone growths, and globules that drip from other worlds like puddles.

The 2019 show *Underbelly* at Museum der bildenden Künste Leipzig grew

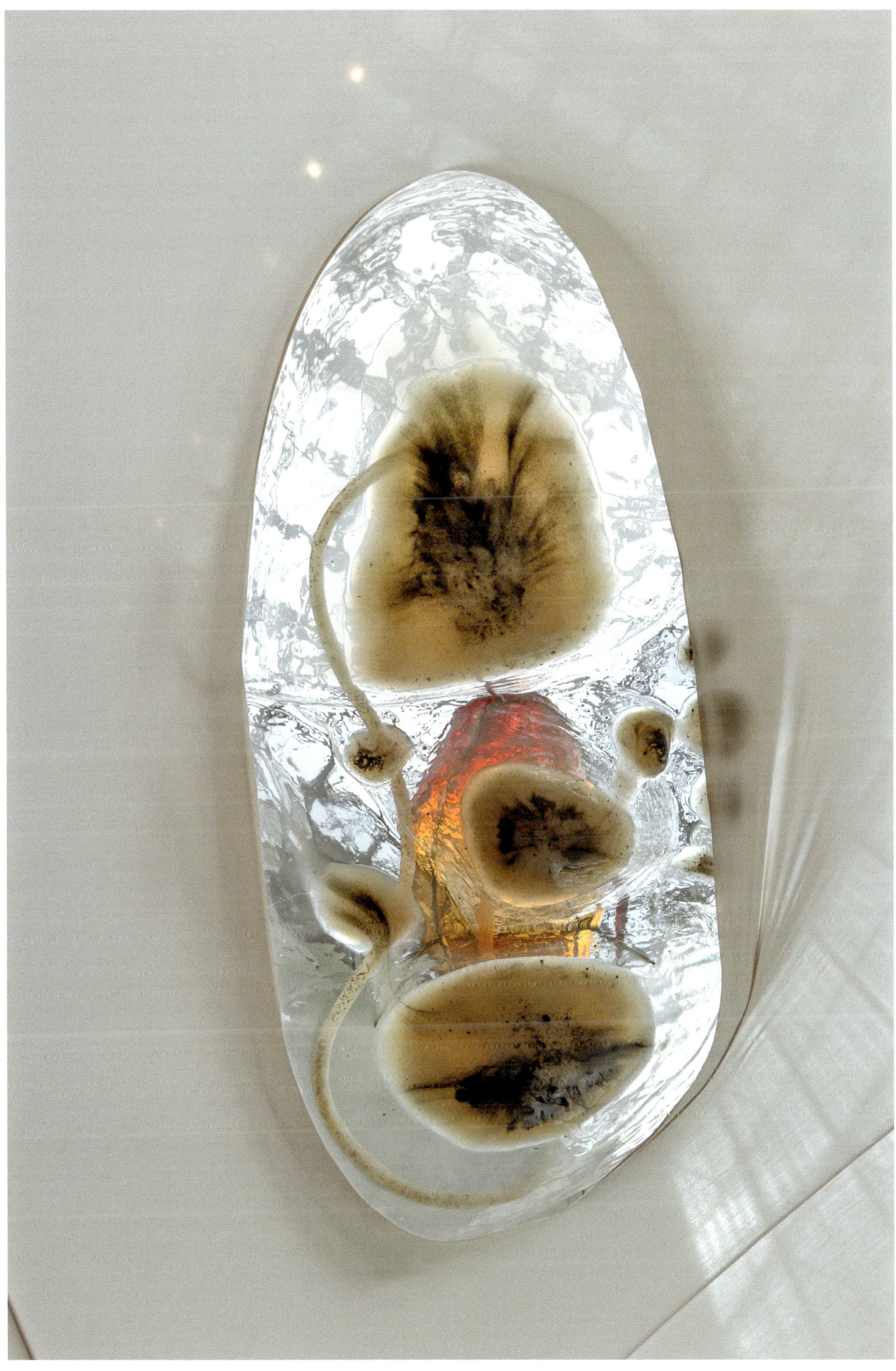

specimens of anatomical creatures—possibly a stereotactic brain biopsy, stomach, or heart valve, we never really know—a *Grey's Anatomy* of glass, chia seeds, and alveoli from a body once living in colorless formaldehyde that was now reanimated as simply *living*. A belle époque from the efforts of anatomizing futuristic life forms. On second or third thought, it was perhaps a moth-eaten coccyx, the fused home of telluric root chakras, so far as I know—meridians and Ayurvedic medicine were never my strong suit. To be rooted emotionally, according to the hyper-pathologizing DSM-5, is a totalizing, metastatic pursuit, yet it's better to get beaten by the whips of familial inheritance first, then thrive later. And thrive emotionally, *Underbelly* did. Pakui Hardware was unyoked and recalcitrant, sidestepping false moves and faulty synapses, building heaven-bound in steely ladders the spine's vertebrae that keep us upright and standing when the going gets tough. What a fruitful mutation! Mutagenic factors find ways around the physical decay of the sphere of trauma, bodily or otherwise, external aggressions whose conditions cause transformations that have psychic implications.

The concept of aesthetic plasticity is crucial from two points of view: it illuminates the social condition that subsumes our bodies while offering an understanding of how the neural substratum can adapt and go *beyond* . . . and it inaugurates the potential of envisaging, through conscious action, transformation of the sociopolitical mind. Activity dependent. We are organisms that must reorganize our brains, bodies, and environments to meet faux bio-mythologies face to face and bring to the fore all the efforts and steps we must take to build alternative existences. Their extraterrestrial memento mori, floating white-sailed paunch, is an iteration of a future reality they'd prefer, shielding our throbbing valves and marrow from predators in the wombs of a chrysalis, rebirthing into an unknown yet safer world. Apathy was never really their strong suit.

Pakui Hardware shows us what we must permanently thrust aside in order to live.

Left wincing and marooned by biological affront, neural pathways alight and septic, viewers of *Underbelly* were offered a

translucent petri dish of future realignments. A world we can actually stomach. And the spine of the argument was this: theirs is a neural realignment that charges us with the somber responsibility of taking control of narratives and the convoluted iterations thereof. Pakui Hardware wants us to know that phenotypic shifts—that is, to descend into modification, pursue net directional or any cumulative change, repopulate the notions of self, trait values, and identity states, spread new genes and alleles all over the fucking place—are *permissible*. Which is to say: Darwinian adaptation. Our bloodied wounds and pus, the sickly, acrid smell of sweat, of organ decay, signify not death but a way to preserve life. *Nothing impedes us*, says Pakui Hardware. Wagging their lost embryonic tail and finger at the gratuitous misconception of stasis, a doctrine that keeps us from evolving, the silver-gated spines and flinching quivers of starless soil and ropes convince us that this barricade is a faux roadblock. Total imposters. The jig is up.

According to the duo, artistic plasticity appears when epigenetics is at work: the otherworldly making and remaking of the totality of an organism in the process of its emerging development. Medical masterpieces are not as distant and abstract as you might think. *Absent Touch* at carlier | gebauer, Berlin, in 2020 further digested the conditions of our environment and innate neurophysiological processes. Back in the surgical room, carefully passing suture needles and sterilized scalpels to one another, the artists planned out the gallery with high precision: tri-arms of blue or yellow surgical lamps; hot-orange glass duodenum; blown-up photography depicting the invasive entry of metal instruments, forceps, tweezers; transparent operating tables draped in pleats of washed apricot cloth. Hospital care is thrice removed from human hands, leaving treatment services to virtual AI carers bought out by vulgar mega-corporations—the immaculate conception of telehealth, telemedicine, and robotic surgery. Immaculate health care conceptions by capitalist proceduralists and clinicians who could—and have already—allayed the swings and sways of raw suppuration without getting their hands dirty.

Literally, but not figuratively. Superior, descending, horizontal, and ascending duodenum parts were scraped and prodded with steely automaton-like arms and diagnostic algorithms in an ethical labyrinth down hospital wings drenched in the stench of ambitious disinfectant. Remote health care technologies in the exhibition took the aesthetics of absence and neglect and blew them up in transcendental pastille installations that were as soft and bewitching as they were cold, sterile, unaffectionate, and (blasphemously) untouched. This is precisely what plasticity is all about: going into spaces that are un-ventured, un-tampered, and ill explored, but don't have to be. The imbalance between organic potentiality and the effects of sedate, environmental stimulations affects our cognitive process as well as generally interferes in ethical sensibilities. Our ability to be involved in the process of mutation that is assailing the biotic features of humans and their activity requires an invasion of cognitive processes in established forms of cognition. Pakui Hardware is not *quaintly* interested in the future ethics of bodies, medicine, robotic operation, and touch. They are vehemently pushing for an assault on uncharted ethical-artistic networks in order to create something affective and associated with meaning that has, thus far, fallen into the hands of nervous activity. Using the aesthetics of absence and un-touch, the duo plié into an exploration of what a material world might be, *could* be, despite charlatan somatic myths around the impotence of plasticity. A most impressive legacy.

Engorged, chafing creative cells take over the Lithuanian Pavilion by our quick-moving dramaturgical creatures and artist Marija Terese Rožanskaitė, who signify life by highlighting what we assume is its insufferable antithetical opponent: Inflammation.[1] Injuring all and injuring well, defiling life with what we can hardly withstand, handling difficulties of the death drive that propels us, pathogens and irritants respond to environmental conditions: food, air, microbes, amputation, myelin. Finding value in inflammation are authors Rupa Marya and Raj Patel, who wrote the book *Inflamed: Deep Medicine and the Anatomy of Injustice*

(2021). The publication has served as an inspiration to Pakui Hardware for its contribution to the Biennale, which takes us, again, on a feverish journey through the human body's digestive, endocrine, circulatory, immune, and nervous systems. This time, they are much more hotheaded, taking a fiery, aggressive approach to the profound injustices at the interstice of bodies, medicine, technology, and capital. Bringing flattened encephalographs back to life, they join Marya and Patel in their continuing examination of violations within political and economic systems. In doing so, they offer a radical new cure for decolonizing the arena: the deep fiery medicine of aesthetic plasticity.

Moving around the space (literally), looking methodically for new pathways in the landscape, are sculptures born of fire themselves: glass and aluminum walk out of hellish flames, untouched. Shadrach, Meshach, and Abednego genuflect before the kinetic sculptures all the way from the Hellenistic period, as Pakui Hardware maps the human nervous system—fragmented, dissolving, epigenetic histories passed down from generation to generation. Pentecostal effigies won't acknowledge lone aesthetic pathways but instead recognize the liberating epigenetic notion that comes as we stage a related, mobile geological intervention. It's very, very provocative. Flamed and inflamed, relative demyelination and damaged synapses are left buying misery as the exhibition impatiently lays the actioned groundwork for possible lanes around the genetic hardships and oppressions archived by our forebears—activity dependent.

Aluminum melts from the ceiling, resembling the corpses of prosthetic extremities, rebuilding the phantom limbs of our ancestors, globules of baroque theater, unmasked and refusing to yield to what was taken away. Frankenstein hybrids that breathe flame and lava, like Baltic dragons, completing bodies in blazing revolution. Contraptions of steel that are reminiscent of orthotic devices in polio patients: archaic, complicated, grotesque, twisted, heterogeneous aesthetic monstrosities. Mongrel plastic soil builds static sculptures in the pavilion that ground themselves in recycled adaptation and agrarian gleaning, learning new

1   An iteration of these ideas were presented as a solo show by Pakui Hardware at the Lithuanian National Museum of Art, Vilnius, in 2023.

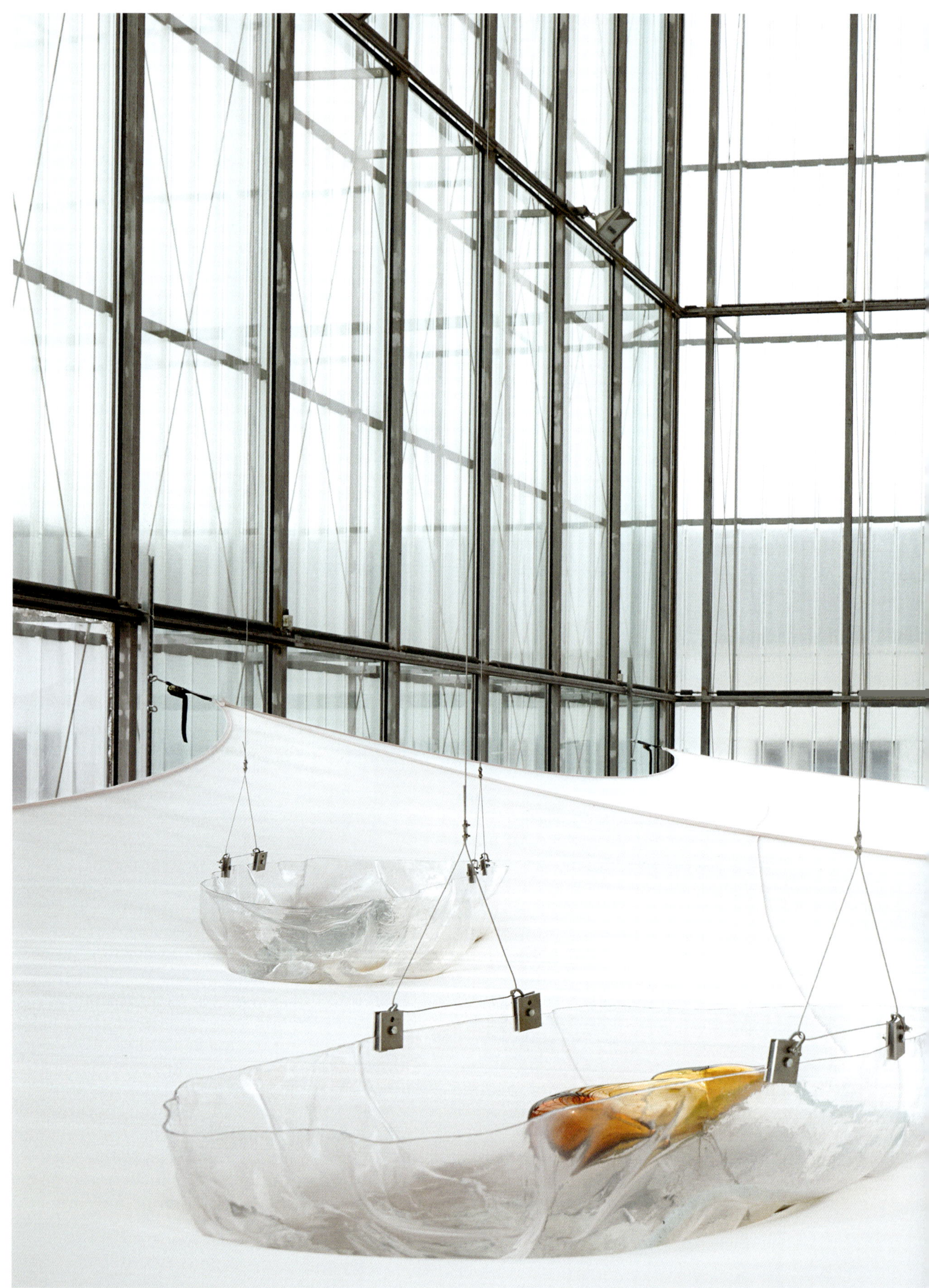

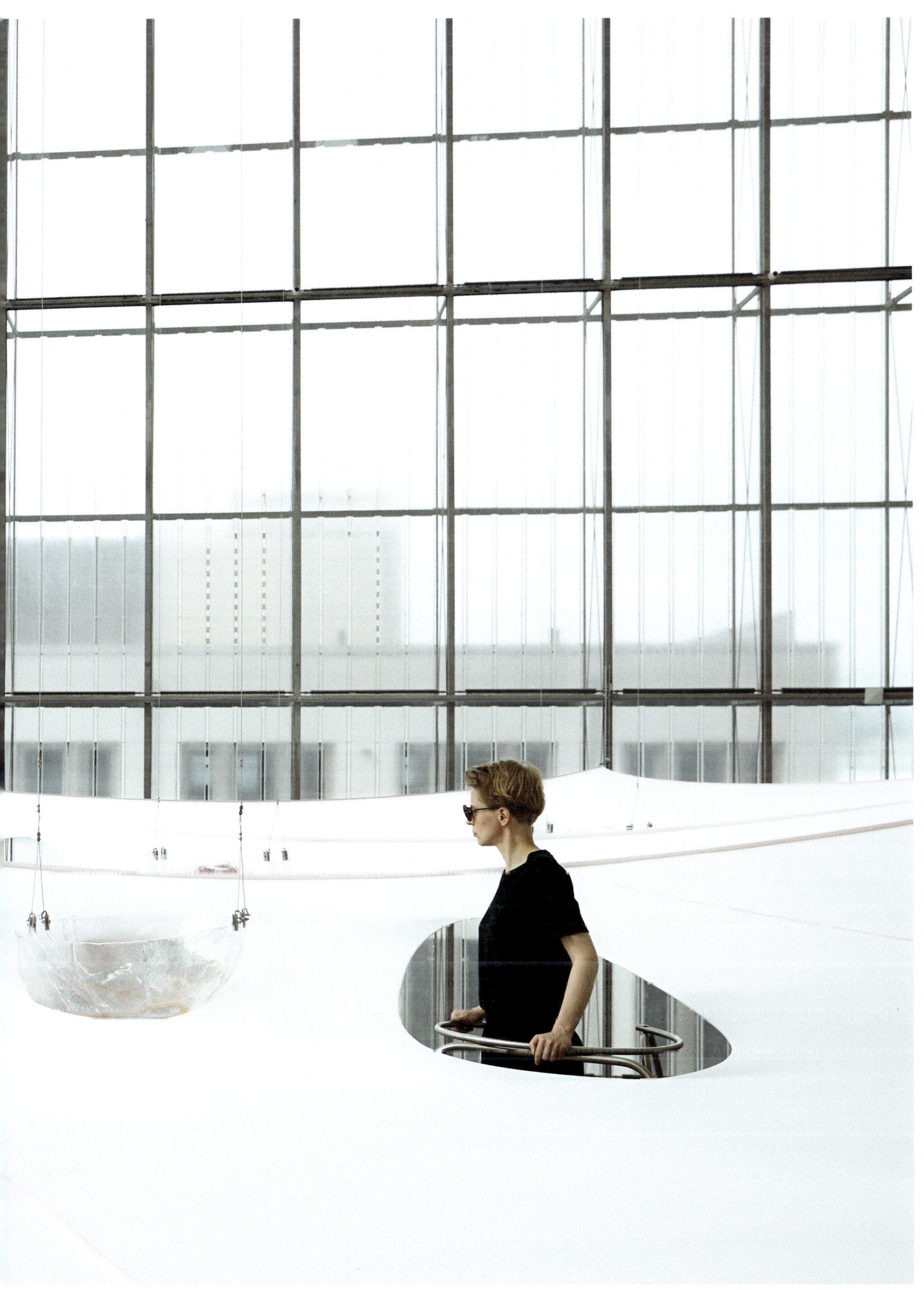

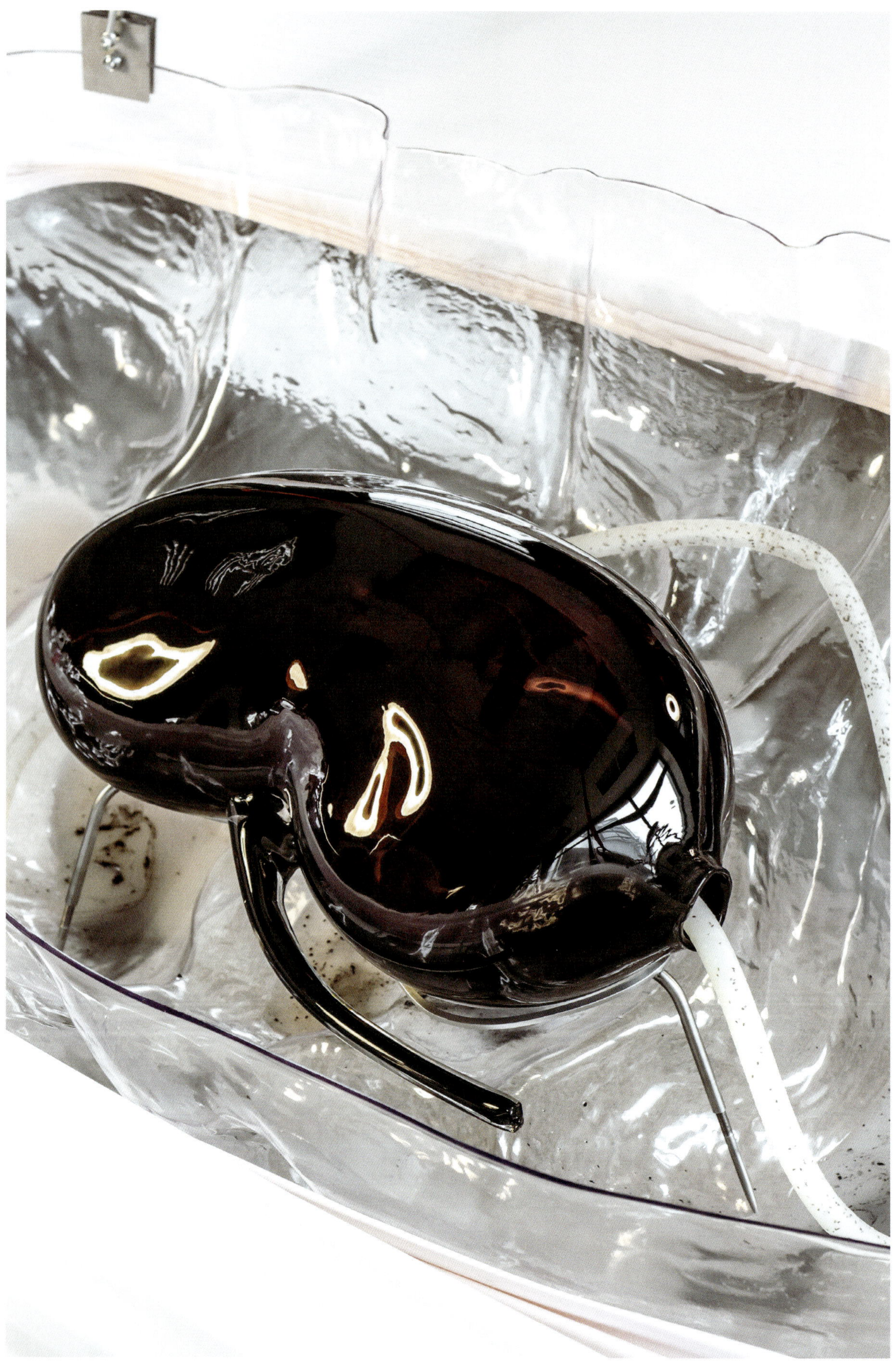

material roles before eventually being re-turned to plastic recycling companies.[2]

Pakui Hardware acts as dramaturge, directing the eye in fixed cortical remapping, showing us that rerouting can look rooted in time and space. Marshaling waning resources and the conscious sense available to them, washed-out glass clings nervously to the prosthetics, dressed in brown and terra-cotta, taking up the occasion to effervesce and ferment in an invisible metabolic process that produces a potent, near-elegiac chemical change. Can *we* crack open healing neurological chemical changes of serotonin, dopamine, anabolic hormones, and thyroxine through unapologetic opportunism, taking the silver scalpel to our genetic inheritance? Pakui Hardware says yes. What a relief.

And bosom friend Marija Teresė Rožanskaitė would likely agree; her paintings of hospitals and noxious landscapes explode the links between bodies and Bolshevism. Soviet systems that *seemed* decadent and marked inexorably from birth, like the archipelago port-wine stain on the skull of Mikhail Gorbachev, eventually proved un-lasting. Coding aesthetic, social genealogies and the powers of horror— a durational performance—Rožanskaitė reconceives all the leverage we have and all the leverage we don't. Paintings of human bodies and cells lament in glassed-capsule frames, ready to crack, a desirous, bifurcated choreography of material bodily labor, self-nominating to rebuild the social architecture of our hyperconnected sea-spongy existence, expunging the notion that our colonial inheritance, politics, and etymology are frozen and congealed. Rožanskaitė and Pakui Hardware's architectural interventions refuse to self-flagellate, take antihistamines to protect themselves from the festering conditions of the environs, or blithely acquiesce to synthetic polymers that tell them, and all of us, that our political codes and possibilities are fixed—total imposters.

Following every whim, Pakui Hardware's oeuvre is heating up, becoming more acidic and temperamental, discoloring bio-myths like an overactive litmus test. The pH balance of their artistic intercessions has shifted over time, with blue litmus paper turning molten red, and neutral pH 7 now a damning 14. It's no coincidence that their initials, PH, reflect a desire to capture and actively reroute the risks of heat and abjection. The corporeal and political benefaction from our relatives is relative, intimately decided by ourselves, respective to the amount we're willing to burrow and change their salient, malleable features—for everyone. An injury to one is an injury to us all.

Here I am at the border of my condition as a living being. Show me what I permanently thrust aside in order to live.

Then let me burn it.

2   The landscape architecture was created by Išora x Lozuraitytė Studio for Architecture. Pakui Hardware has collaborated with the Išora x Lozuraitytė Studio for Architecture in a number of other exhibitions, including *Underbelly* (2019), *Virtual Care* (2021) and *Vanilla Eyes* (2016) among others.

Inga Lāce

X-Rays of Our Society:
Marija Teresė Rožanskaitė and Pakui Hardware

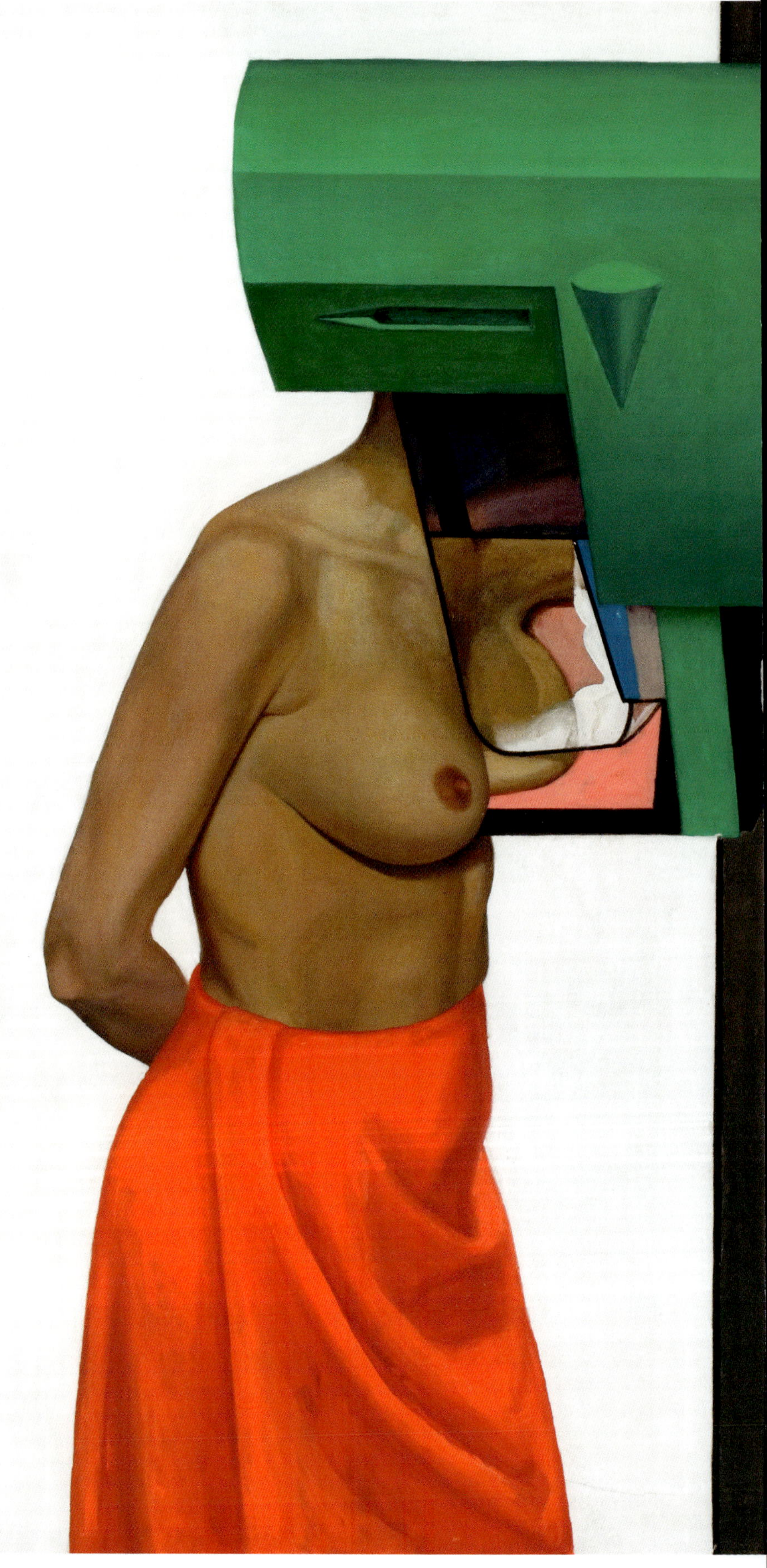

↑ Marija Teresė Rožanskaitė, *X-Ray Therapy*, 1977. Oil on canvas, 140 × 160 cm
Photo: Antanas Lukšėnas. Courtesy the Lithuanian National Museum of Art, Vilnius

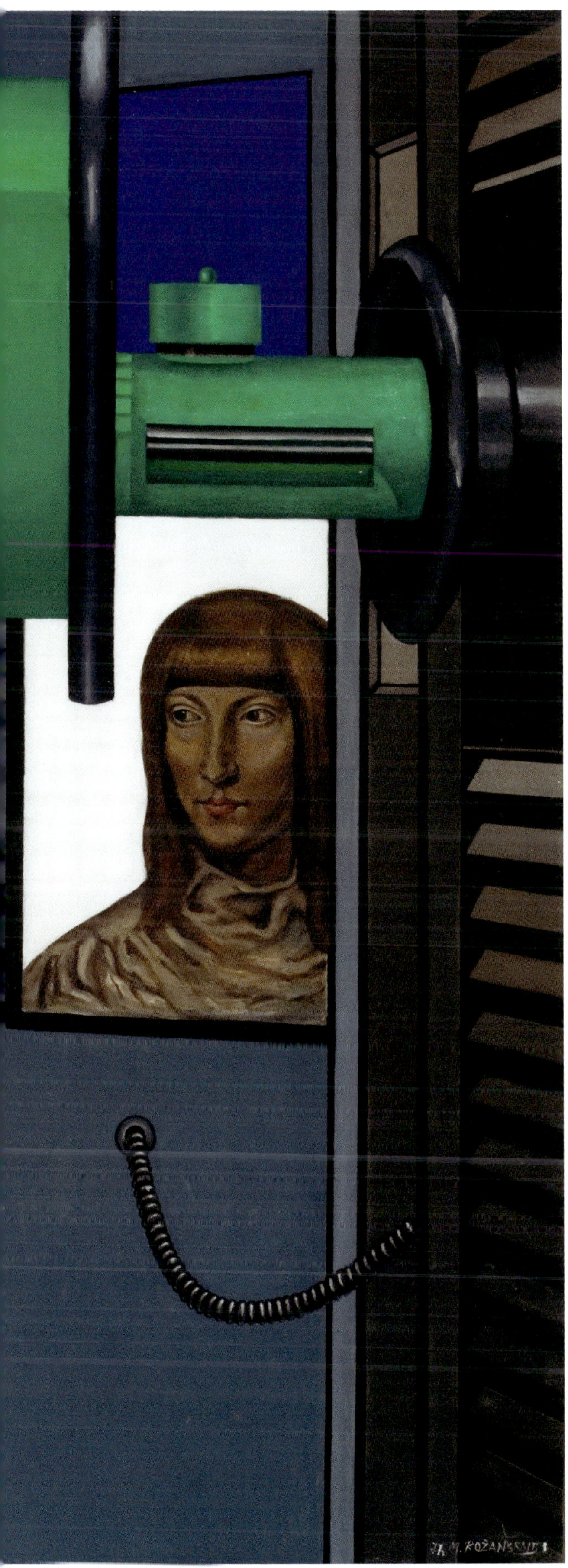

The first demonstration of X-ray equipment in Vilnius took place in April 1896, just a year after the discovery of X-rays in Wurzburg, Germany, by Wilhelm Conrad Röntgen (which had occurred somewhat accidentally, as many scientific advances do). Soon, pioneering radiology units were opened in Vilnius and Kaunas, the new science entered medical education, and new applications were developed.[1] X-rays produce images of internal tissues, bones, and organs through invisible electromagnetic energy beams. Used to diagnose tumors or bone injuries, they remain a cornerstone of modern medicine.

The X-ray procedure and the technical equipment necessary for it, as well as the patient and doctor and the X-ray image itself, feature prominently in several works by the renowned Lithuanian artist Marija Teresė Rožanskaitė, who developed an interest in medicine in the late 1960s. She pursued this engagement throughout her career, later moving to questions of old age, for instance sickness and loneliness as viewed through the lens of alienating hospital wards. Her series of hospital- and medicine-related work coincided with the general techno-utopian mood of the Soviet Union, where artists' research trips into the spaces of science and industry, like the facilities of nuclear reactors or factories, were commonplace, and served the Soviet propaganda program.

While the Nikita Khrushchev era (1953–64) brought changes into the dynamic of the Cold War, namely a renewed investment into scientific achievements and a more liberalized environment for art, the following moment under Leonid Brezhnev saw economic progress slowly entering stagnation. The positive propaganda did not cease, however. For decades, the Communist Party was self-congratulatory, proclaiming that socialist medicine was the best in the world while in the meantime failing to invest adequately in health care. Short life expectancy was a reality of a system that broadly disregarded the needs of Soviet citizens. Rožanskaitė did not praise the achievements of Soviet medicine, even though she did treat it as a subject. Her work transcended the logic of representation of success and introduced tension into the procedure hall and the frailty of the examined body.

1. Algirdas Basevičius and Saulius Lukoševičius, *Lithuanian Radiologists' Association: A Historical Glimpse* (Vienna: European Congress of Radiology, 2017).

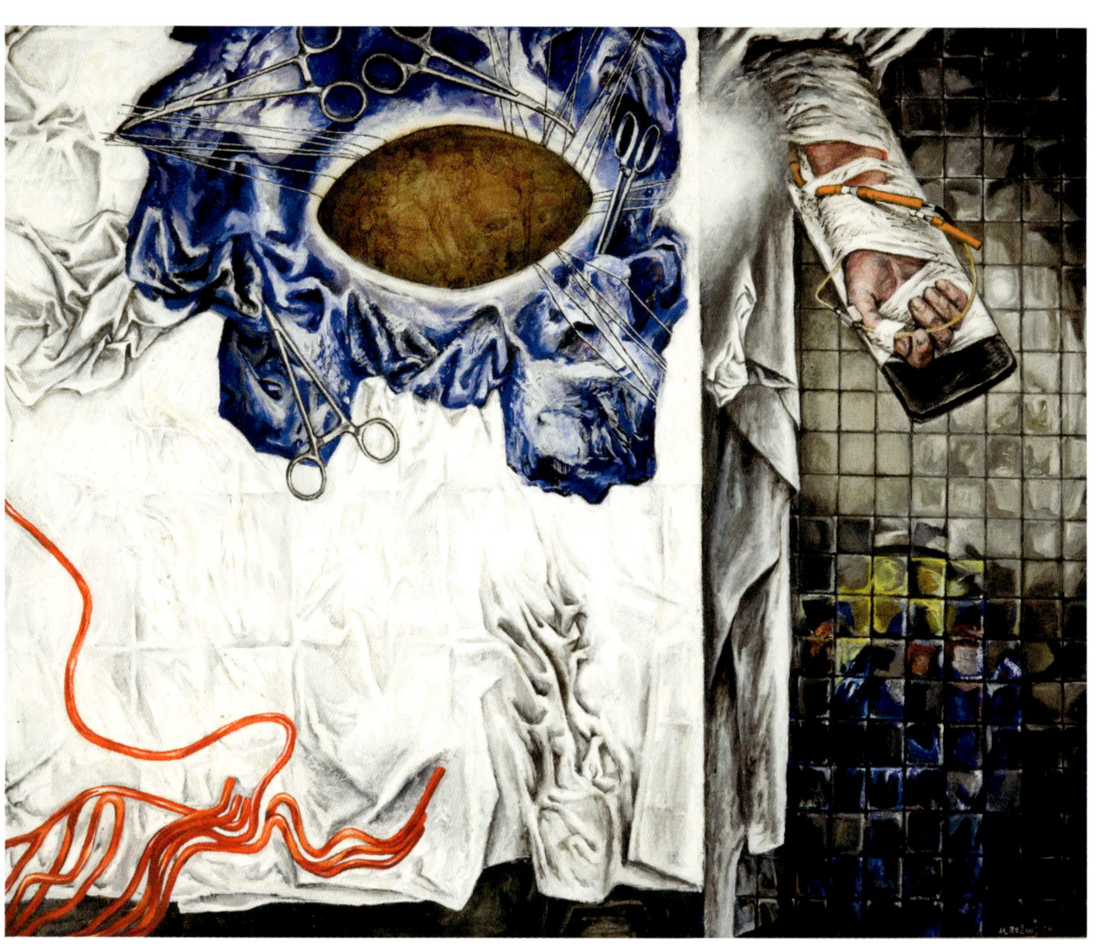

↑   Marija Teresė Rožanskaitė, *Heart Surgery II*, 1974. Oil on cardboard, 158 x 190 cm
Photo: Kęstutis Stoškus. Courtesy the MO Museum

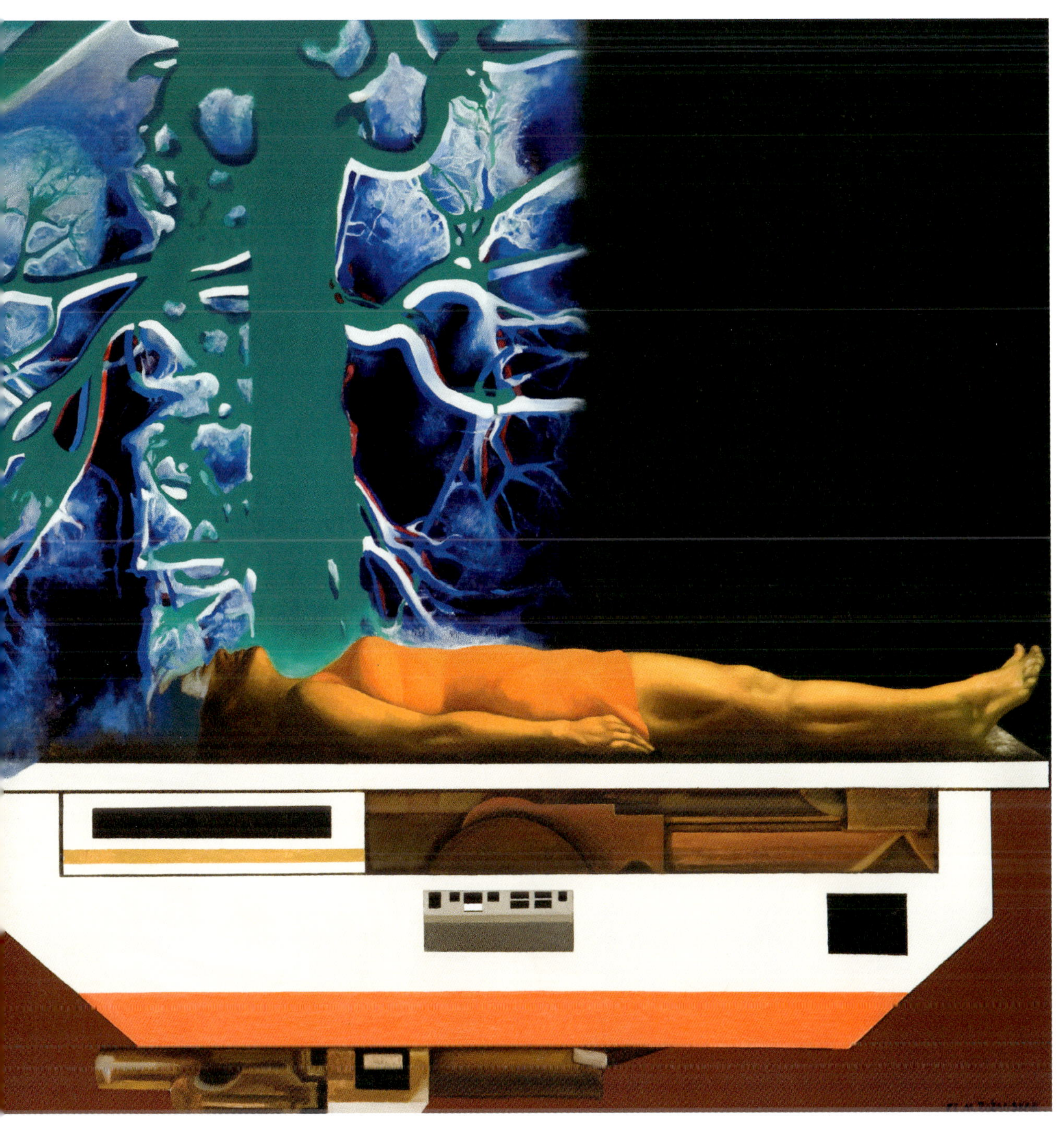

 ↑ Marija Teresė Rožanskaitė, *X-Ray*, 1977. Oil on canvas, 150 x 170 cm
Photo: Kęstutis Stoškus. Courtesy the MO Museum

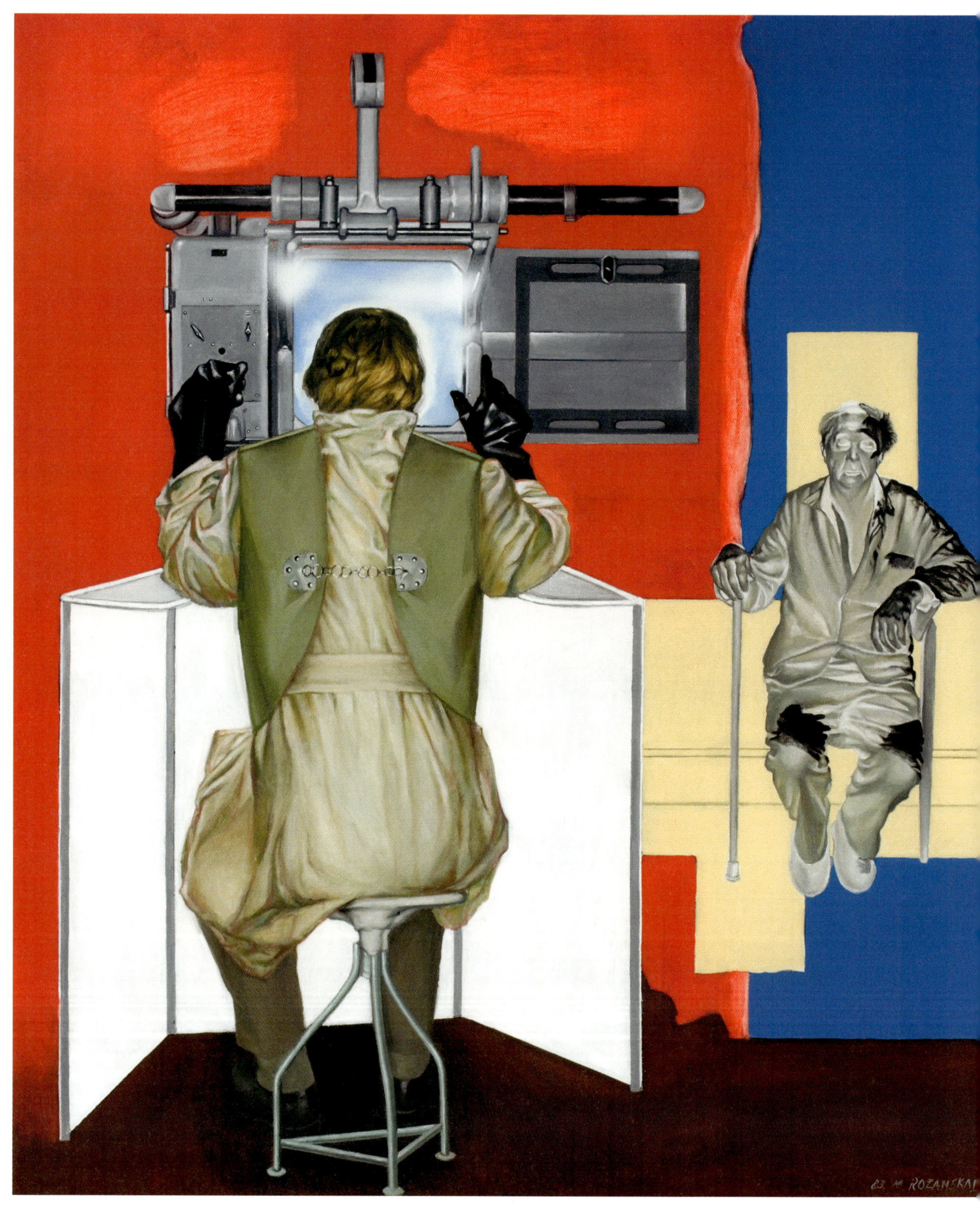

↑ Marija Teresė Rožanskaitė, *X-Ray Room*, 1983. Oil on canvas, 150 × 130 cm
Photo: Vidmantas Ilčiukas. Courtesy the Lithuanian National Museum of Art, Vilnius

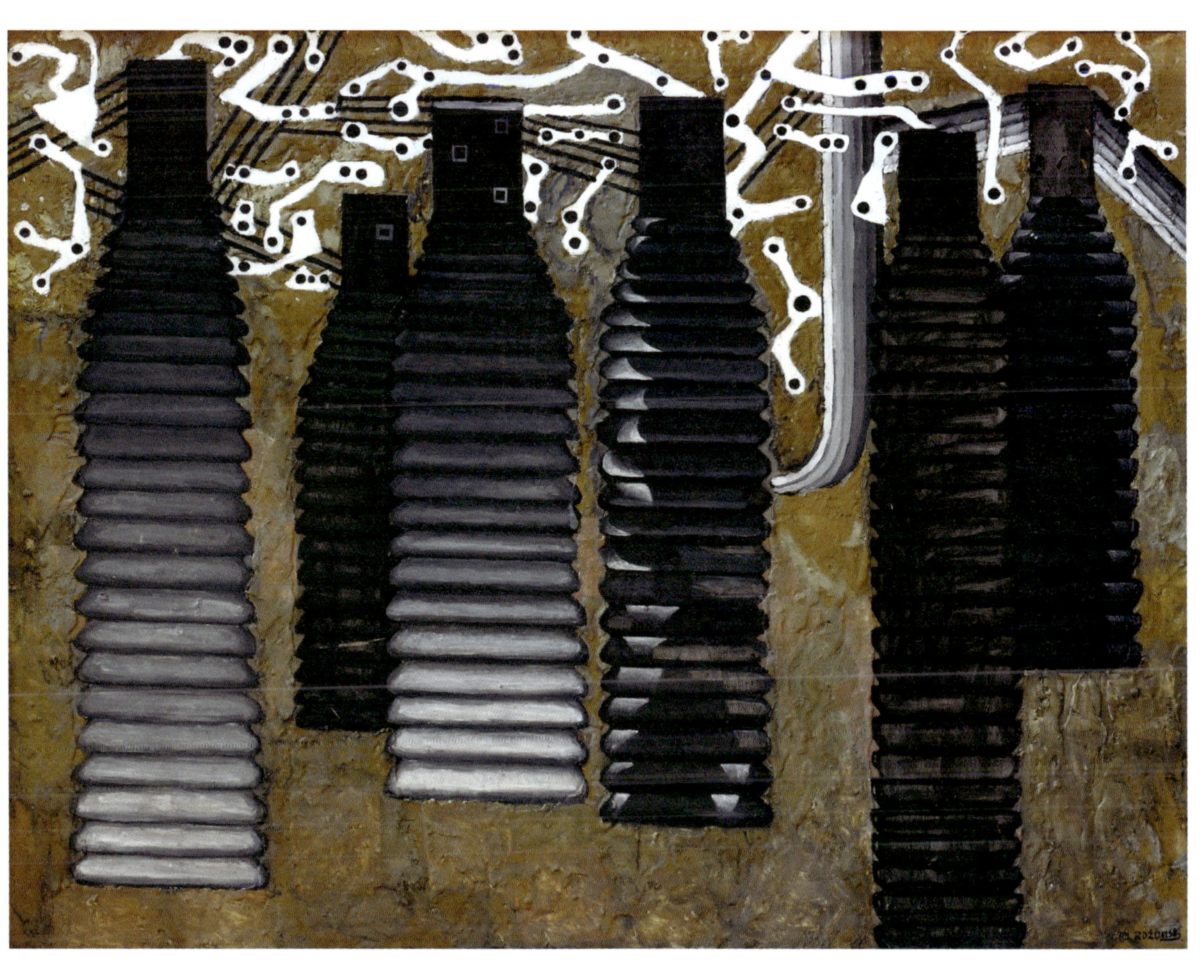

↑ Marija Teresė Rožanskaitė, *Industrial Landscape*, 1970. Oil on cardboard, mixed technique, 120 × 150 cm
Photo. Vidmantas Ilčiukas. Courtesy the artist's family

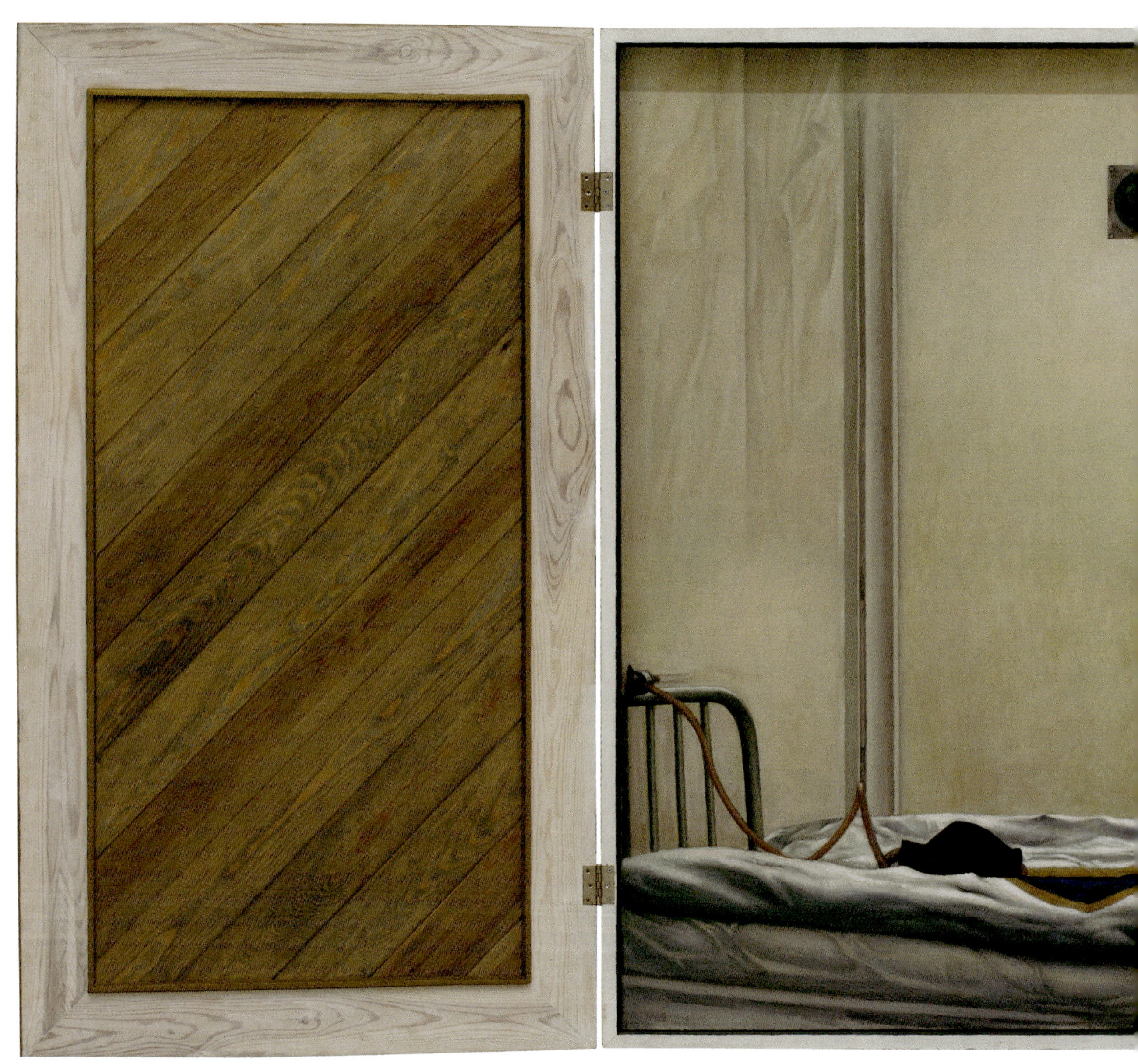

 ↑ Teresė Marija Rožanskaitė, *Bed. Triptych*, 1987. Oil on canvas, wood, 144.5 × 130 cm
Photo: Antanas Lukšėnas. Courtesy the Lithuanian National Museum of Art

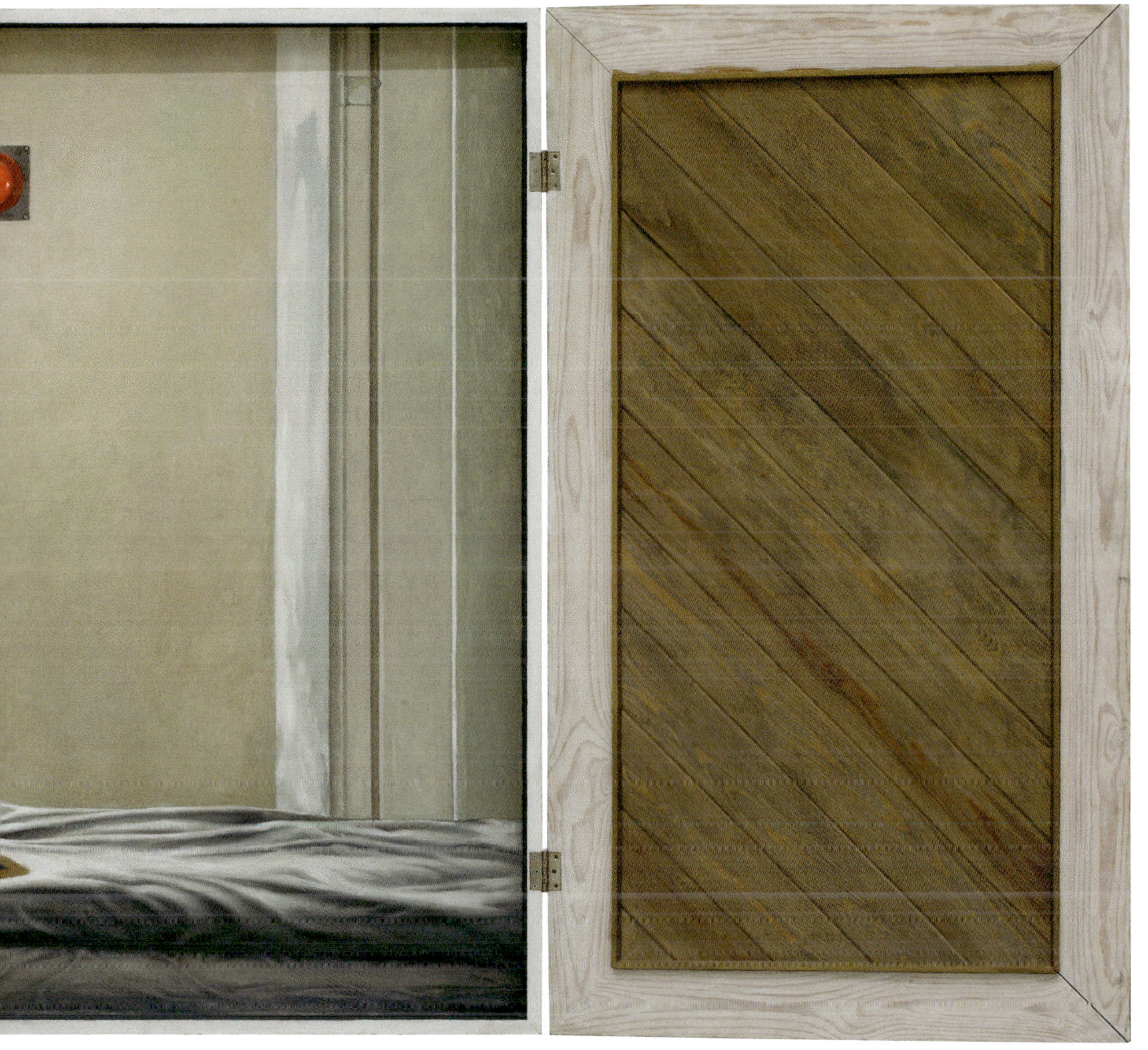

Her series *X-Ray* (1977–1983) highlights an important part of the medical system—diagnostics—emphasizing the encounter between patient and doctor, and their mutual entanglement with the technical equipment. In *X-Ray* (1977), a young woman is lying on a table undergoing the procedure. Above her is an enlarged fragment of her X-ray photograph. Sinking in on her body, the depiction looks like a strange dream she may be having involving a shadow of a tree, or it could indeed be a lung's branching into small capillaries. Medical information is a language understood by doctors who will translate it into health or disease, the borders between which will depend on the body politics of the moment.

Another two works from the *X-Ray* series again bring forward the patient-doctor relationship, emphasizing the power dynamics between layperson and expert. In *X-Ray Therapy* (1977), a woman with her head in the machine is half naked while the coldly analytic gaze of another woman rests observantly on her nude, vulnerable body, *X-Ray Room* (1983) concerns a doctor examining an X-ray while a patient sits uneasily nearby. In both, the patient is clearly uncomfortable, insecure, while the gaze and the body language of the doctor are assertive, stressing once more the power of scientific knowledge over bodies. The X-ray is a photographic apparatus, but it is scanning the body much more deeply than any photograph ever would, burrowing under the skin.

Heart Surgery I and *II* (1974) depict operations taking place within a scenography of a draped cloth. The red-blood-filled tubes cross the drapery in one corner of *Heart Surgery II*, while a hand reaches out in the other. The heart, like a wound in the center of the operation, is a spheric-looking hole—a dark brown opening surrounded by blue cloth and medical scissors, with large stitches stemming from the wound, placed rhythmically, almost decoratively. With a clear viewpoint from above, both paintings remind us of operating theaters used for medical education, yet here they abstract rather than reveal the injured bodies or the medical procedures themselves.

Even though sometimes absent from Rožanskaitė's spaces, people and their

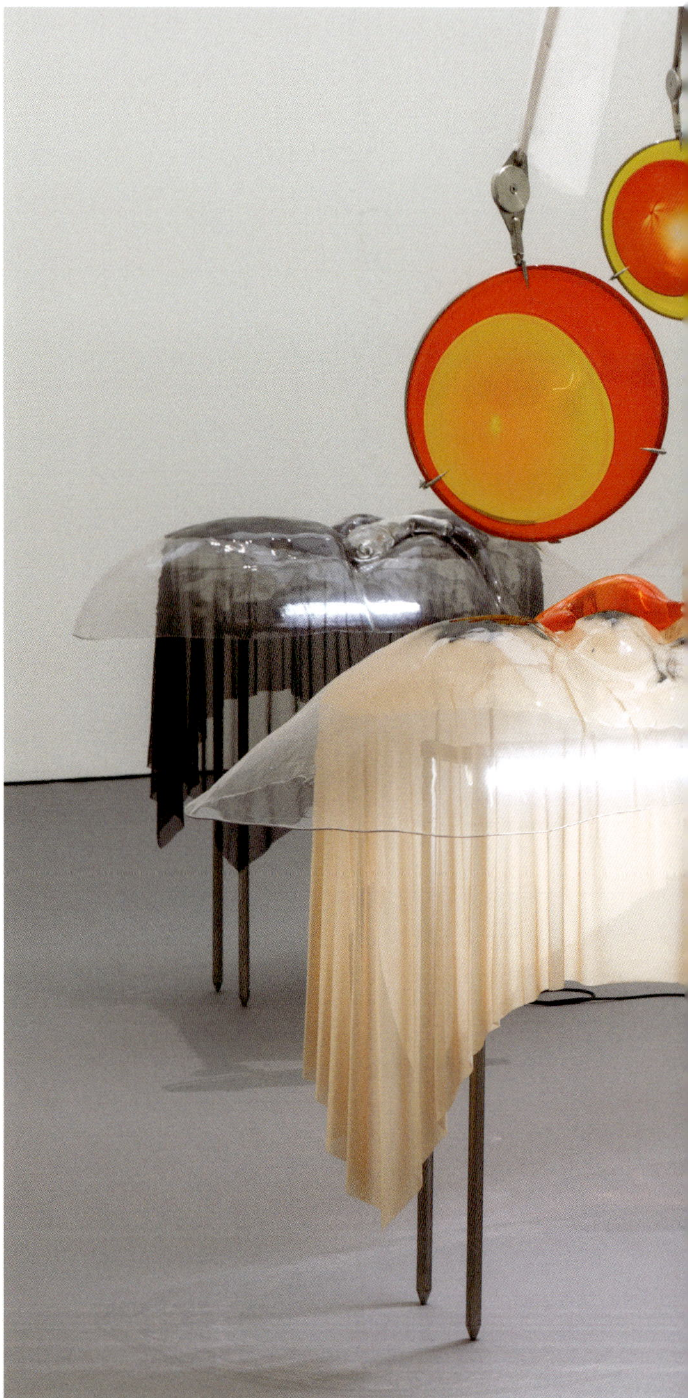

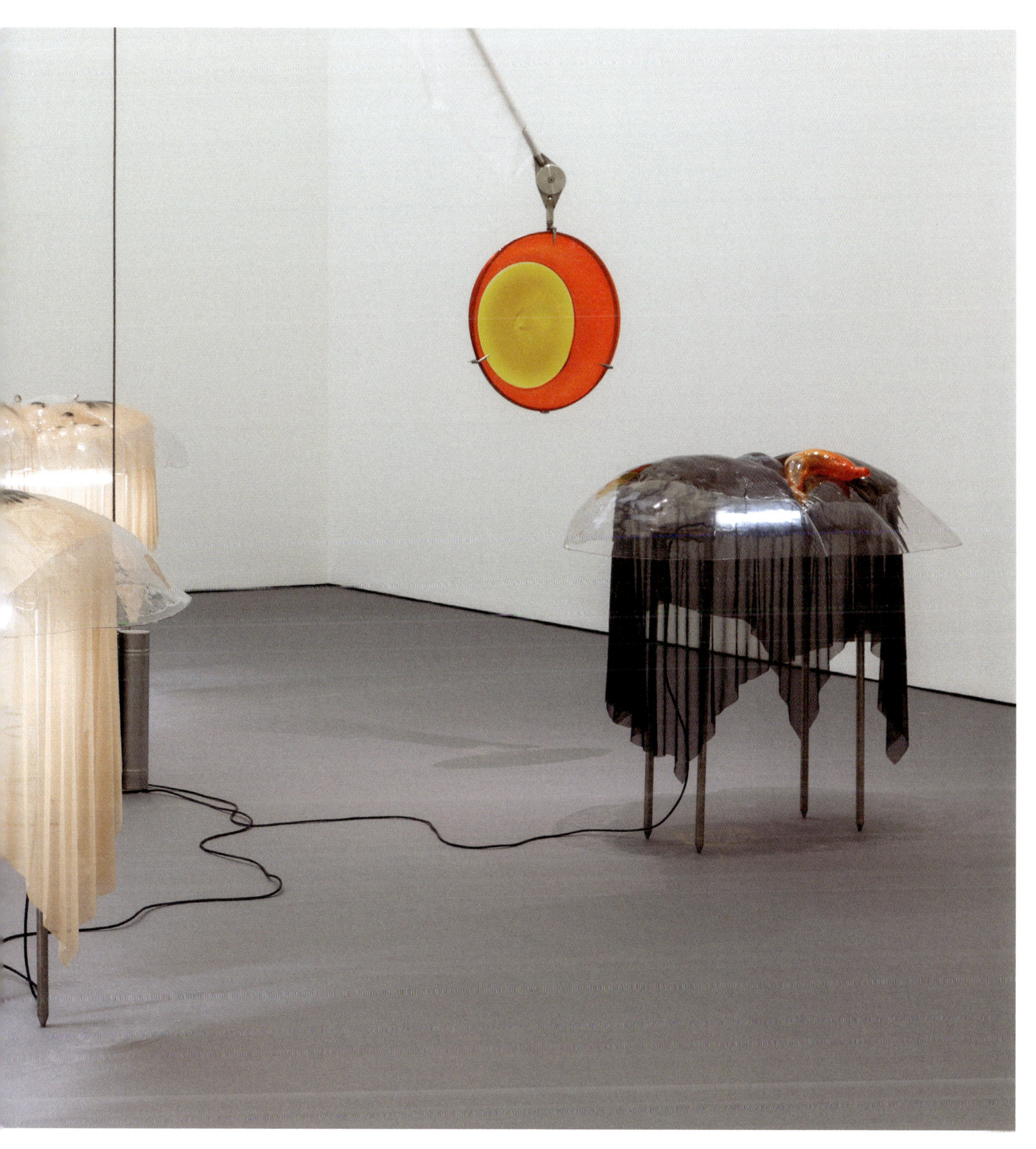

 ↑→ Pakui Hardware, *Virtual Care*, 2021. Installation view, BALTIC Centre for Contemporary Art, Gateshead, England, 2021
Photo: Rob Harris. Courtesy the Lithuanian National Museum of Art, Vilnius

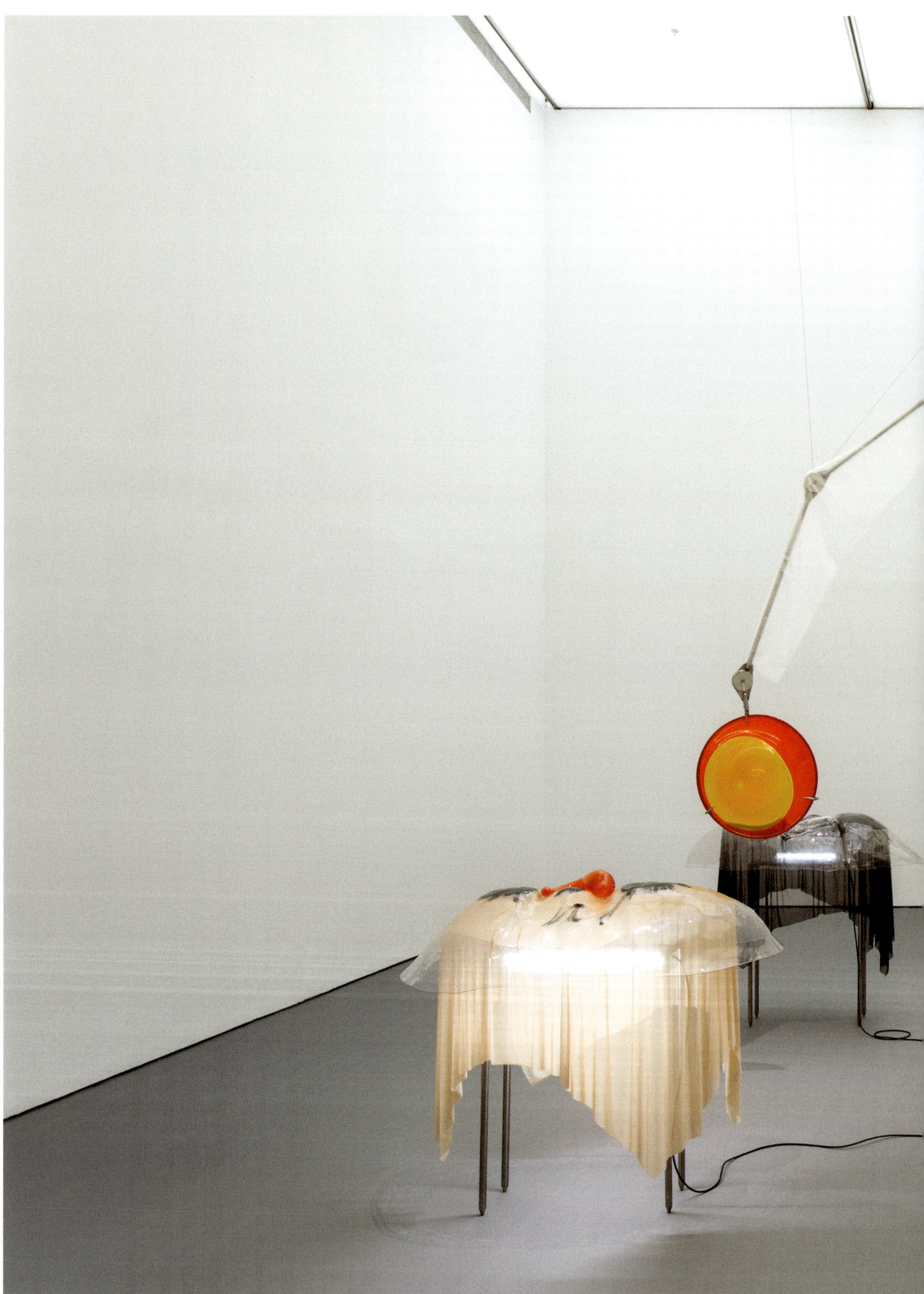

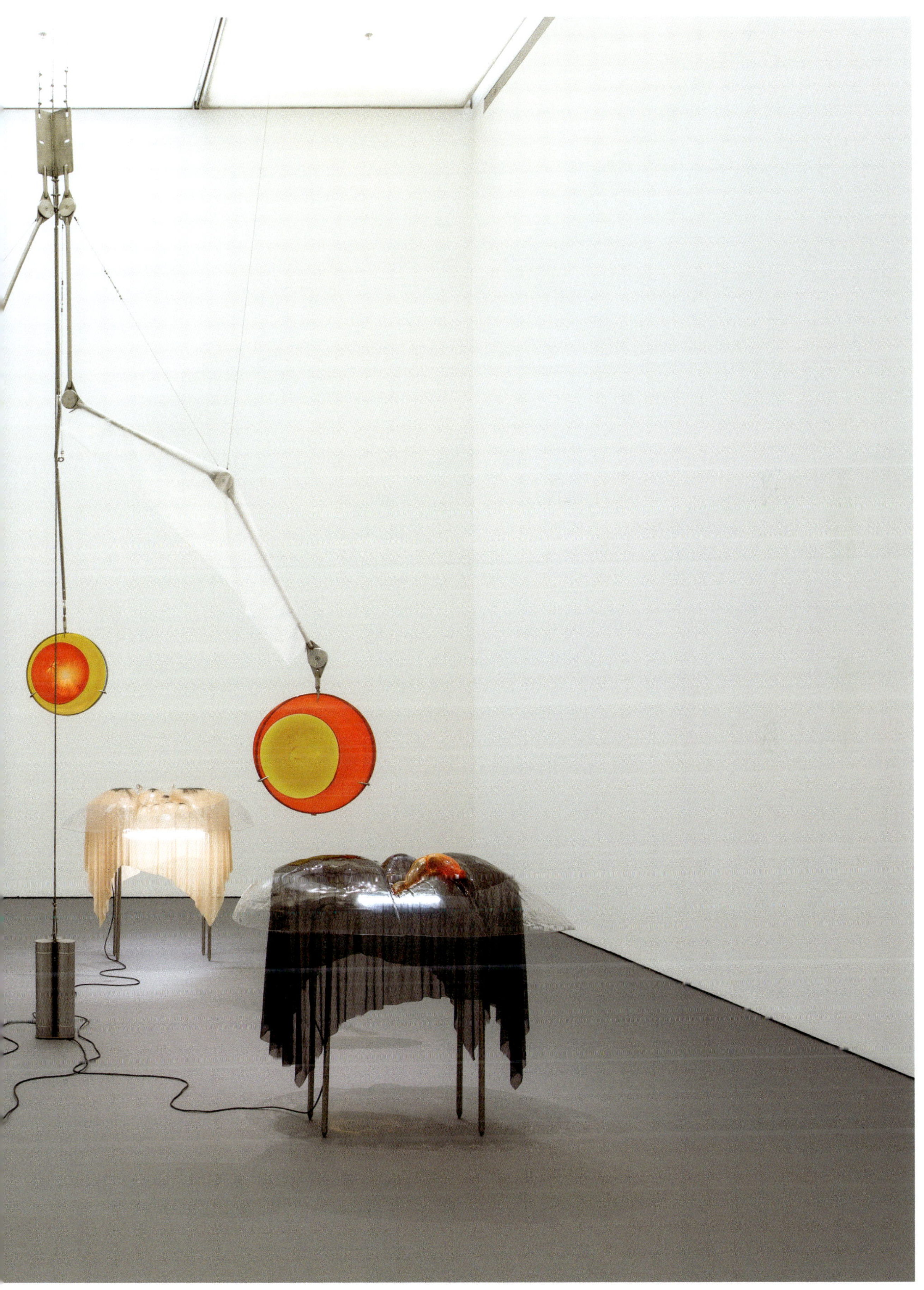

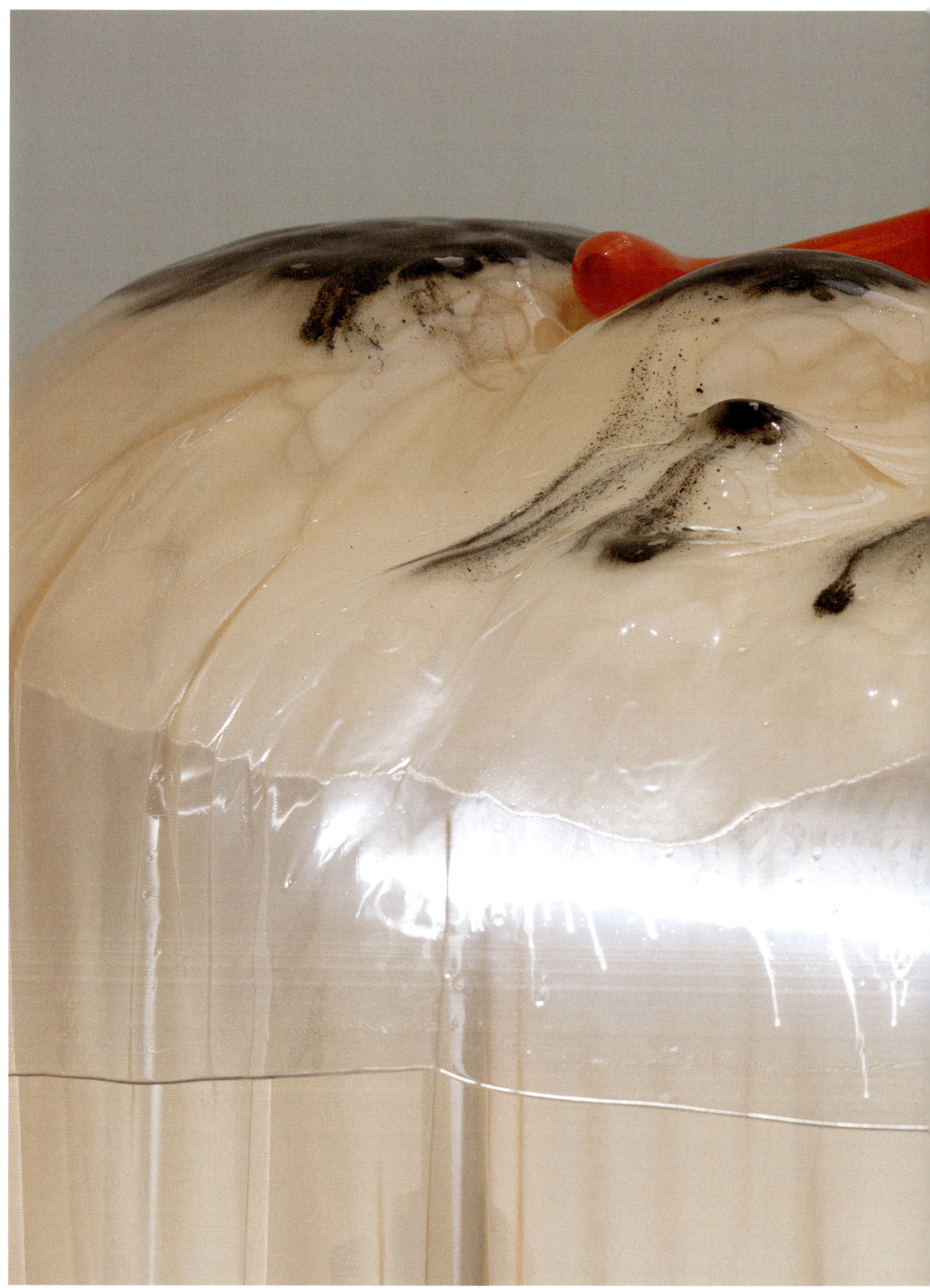

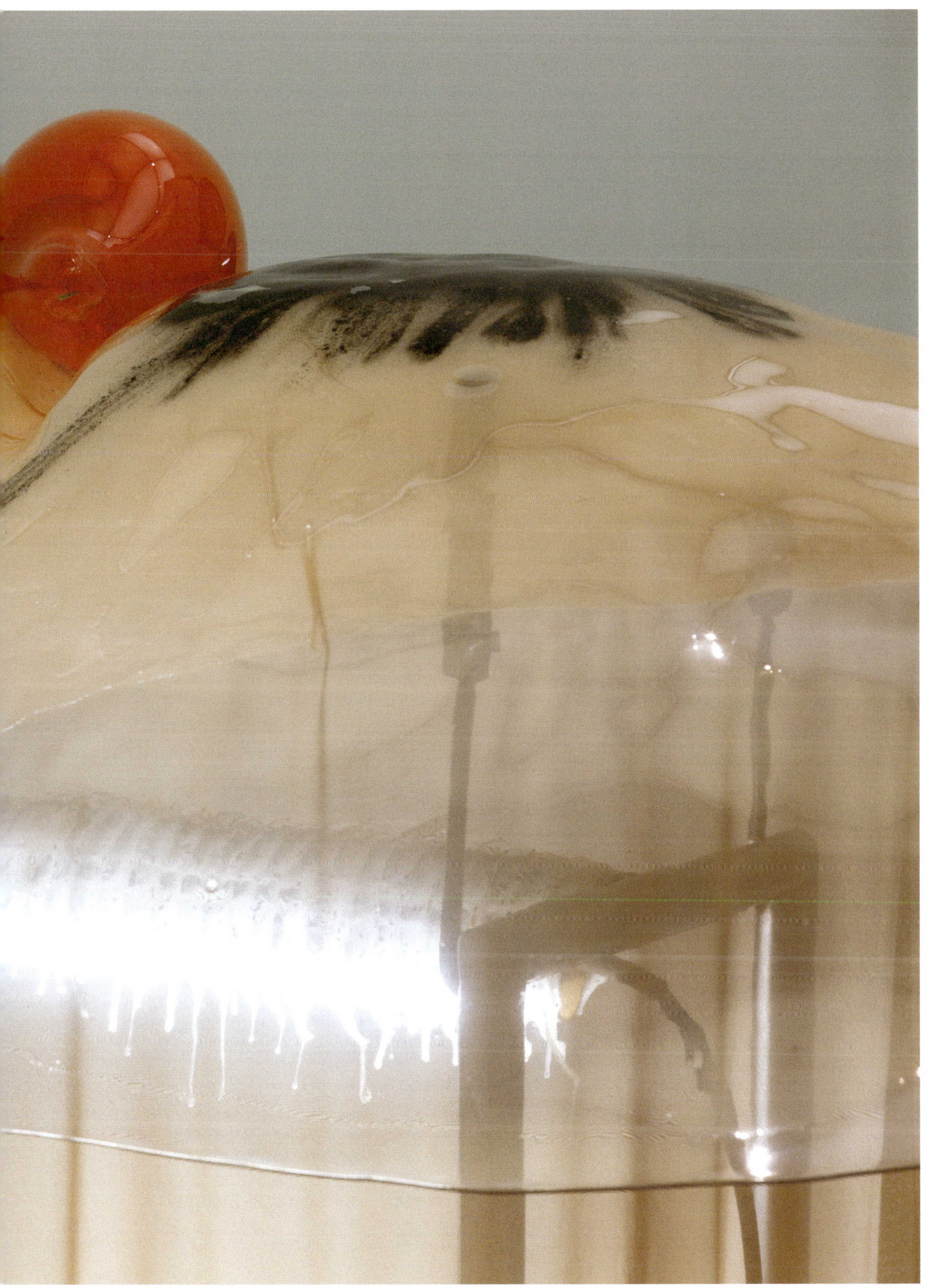

relationships with each other or with technology were of utmost importance for her—how the patient subjects their body to the doctor's observation and that of the machine, as well as the distancing alienation created by medical equipment, and at the same time its inevitable entanglement with bodies. The simultaneous hope and helplessness in her work is likely immediately recognizable given our own personal histories of doctors' appointments. Through the fragility of the human body, Rožanskaitė commented on the larger ills of Soviet society, both the precarity of the medical system and the life and freedoms of the citizens; the bureaucracy of life was comparable to the waiting room of a hospital, and the whole socialist experiment to an operation hall.[2] Rožanskaitė, as a child, was sent to Siberia with her family. Her mother lost a child on the way, and many people didn't return at all. This experience of death and survival adds another layer to the ailing bodies she depicted—failing, yet yearning to be cured.

Rožanskaitė's paintings of medical spaces and operations served as inspiration for the Lithuanian artist duo Pakui Hardware (founded by Neringa Černiauskaitė and Ugnius Gelguda in 2014) in the trilogy of projects *Virtual Care* (2021), *Absent Touch* (2020) and *The Host* (2021), all of which forefront the contemporary implications of care and its intersections with technology. Pakui Hardware has long been interested in biological processes such as metabolism, and the growing ubiquity of medical enhancements in our techno-capitalist world.

Absent Touch transformed the gallery environment into a kind of surgery room in which the humans we ordinarily imagine inhabiting it—doctors, nurses, the patient—were nowhere to be seen. Attached to three metallic "hands" reaching out from the ceiling were round, colored-glass sculptures resembling enlarged examination mirrors or surgical lamps. Where the table with the patient was supposed to be, one saw a set of stands relying on metallic "legs," coated first with a layer of fabric, then covered with plastic shields. A fragile glass object rested carefully in the folds of each of the covers. Not human for sure, but not fully animal or technological either, these installations remained an ambiguous yet recognizable presence. We don't need to see scissors to imagine a cut. It can be done with a laser, programmed digitally without a blink of real flesh. Not seeing limbs or even instruments, we can still imagine an operating room. But a much broader set of procedures can be implied in the spaces that Pakui Hardware creates, collapsing the human, the nonhuman animal, and the technological.

Through varied materials, shapes, and colors, the work also brings forward the tension—purely materially and associatively—between the warmth and fragility, and the mechanical coldness, existing simultaneously in medical spaces. The metal shapes of "hands" and "legs" next to the crafty imprecision of the glass objects, fragile and warm, is but one example. The room itself created a sense of encounter akin to that of the hospital, where the idea of care and warmth is rarely manifested in the actual rooms or medical equipment involved in the care-giving processes. This alienation, however, is blurrier today, according to the researcher Jeannette Pols in her 2012 study *Care at a Distance: On the Closeness of Technology*. It is rather that which is readily technologically accessible that will serve as care instead of the warmth of a physical encounter, if the former is unattainable. But is it really so, Pakui Hardware still inquire.[3]

Another important aspect of medical spaces, aside from the architecture and buildings themselves, are the views on healing. When scholars started to analyze the nineteenth-century invention of the modern hospital, they posited a crucial change: a shift from care to cure. The modern hospital was dedicated to curing the sick, whereas today, health care reformers are advocating for a shift from cure to care.[4] This shift is readily present in the work of Pakui Hardware through the virtual aspects of care. Opened at the peak of the pandemic, in November 2020, *Absent Touch* raised an important issue, namely the absence of touch that we were all encouraged to practice. Absence, of course, was present already before the pandemic and entered Pakui Hardware's work through their research into the technologies of telemedicine. This form of health care originated in the

2.   See Aistė Paulina Virbickaitė, http://www.mmcentras.lt/kuriniai/sirdies-operacija-ii/2587.
3.   See Laima Kreivytė, *Marija Teresė Rožanskaitė, Rentgenogramos/X-Rays* (Vilnius: Lithuanian Art Museum, 2013), 19.
4.   Pakui Hardware (Neringa Černiauskaitė), "Hesitant Hand," mumok.at, https://www.mumok.at/en/blog/pakui-hardware-hesitant-hand; David Theodore, "From Care to Cure and Back Again: David Theodore," *e-flux Architecture*, September 2021, https://www.e-flux.com/architecture/treatment/410320/from-care-to-cure-and-back-again/.

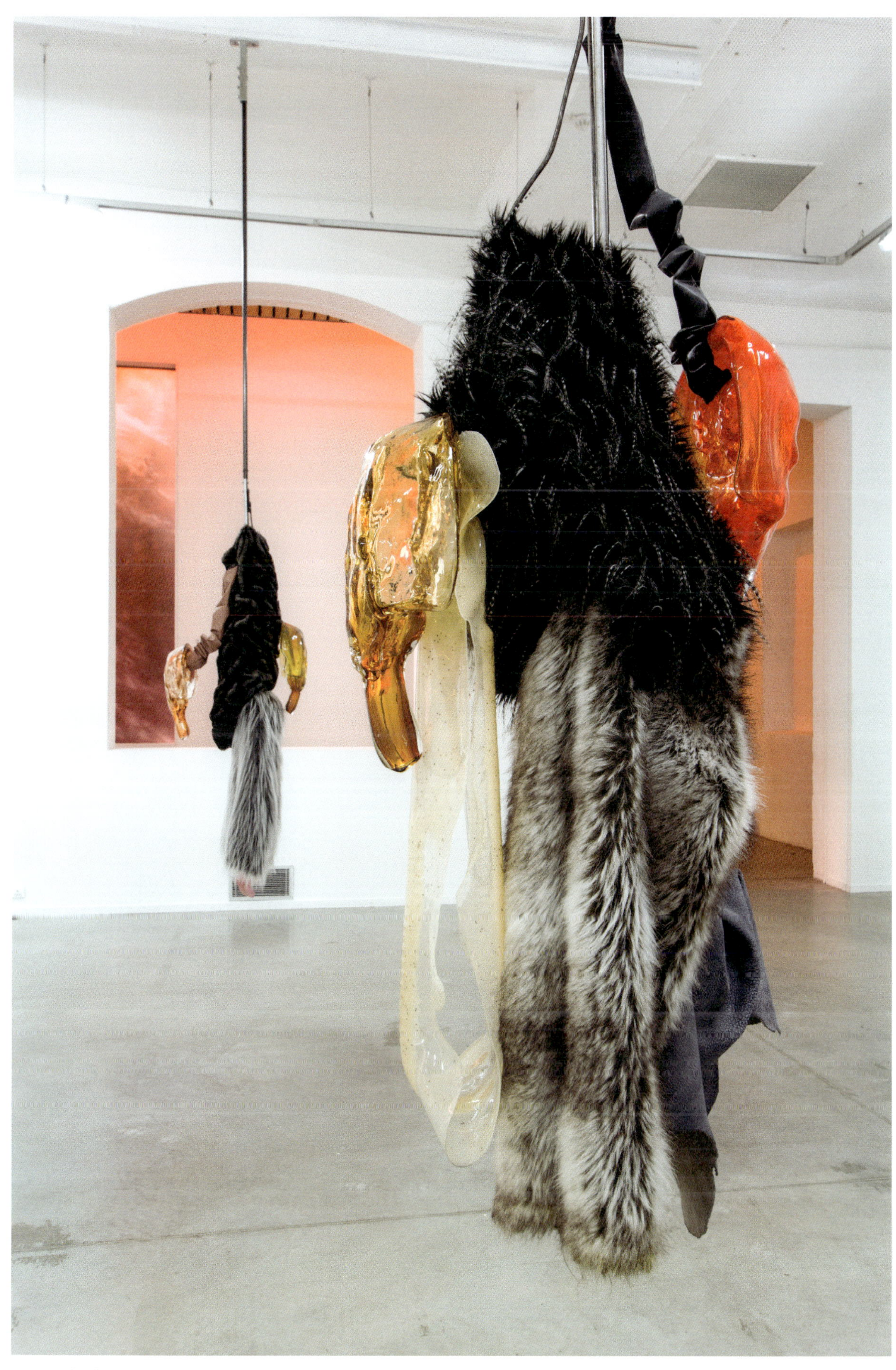

 ↑ Pakui Hardware, *Extrakorporal*, 2018. Installation view, MO.CO., Montpellier, France, 2019
Photo: Ugnius Gelguda. Courtesy the artists and carlier | gebauer, Berlin & Madrid

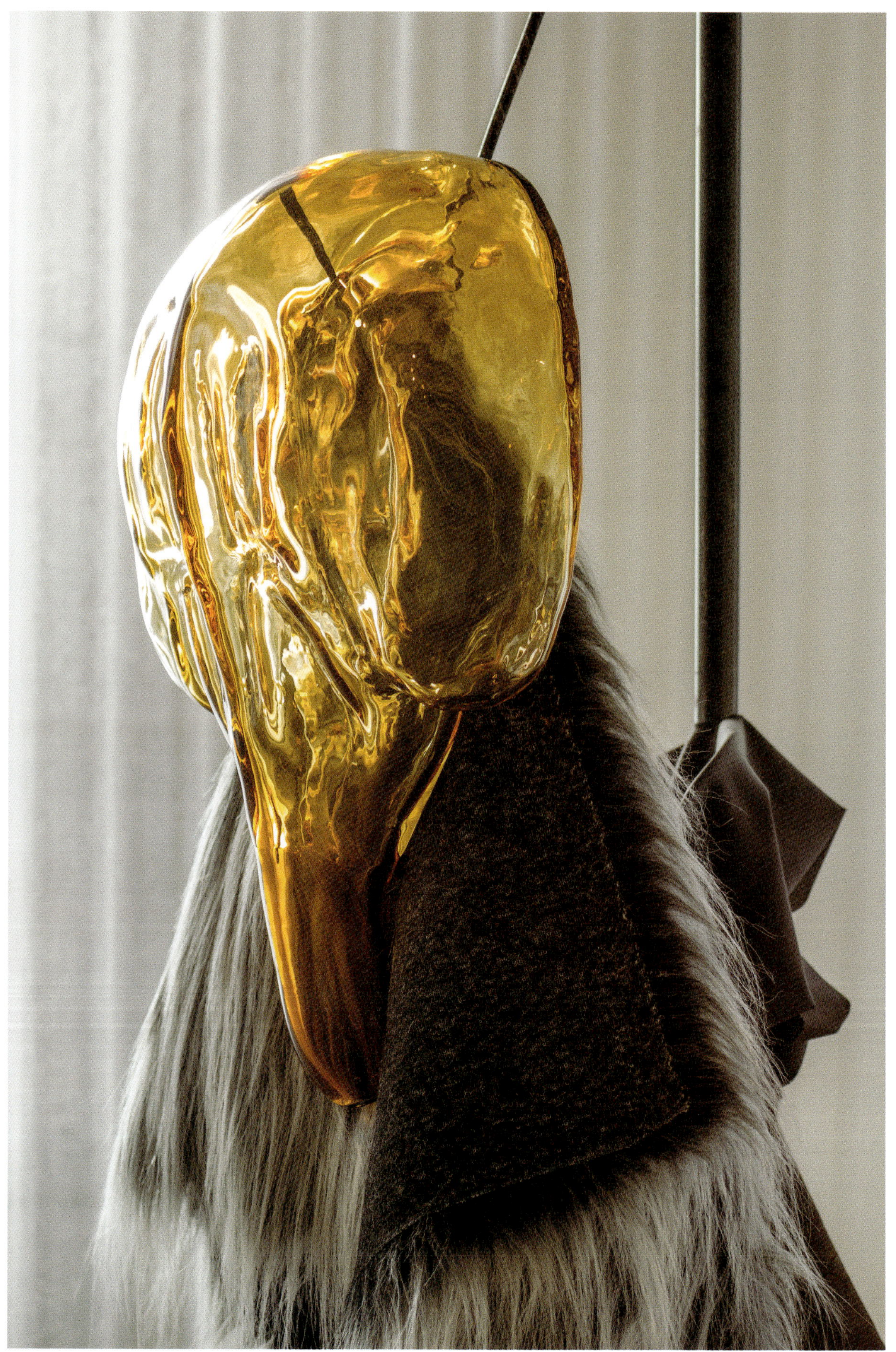

 ↑→ Pakui Hardware, *Extrakorporal*, 2018. Installation view, Kunstverein Bielefeld, Germany, 2018
Photo: Ugnius Gelguda. Courtesy MO Museum, Vilnius

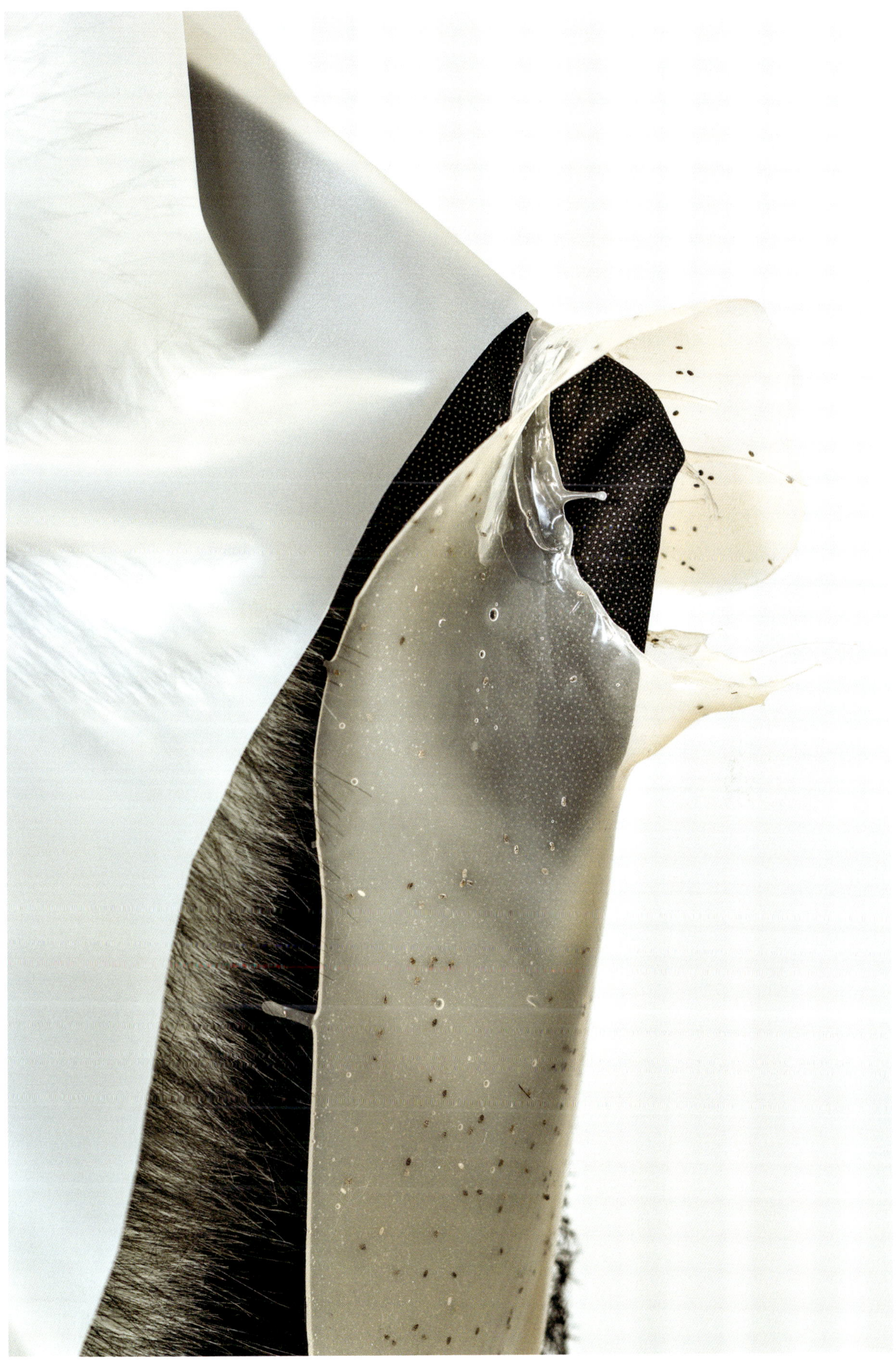

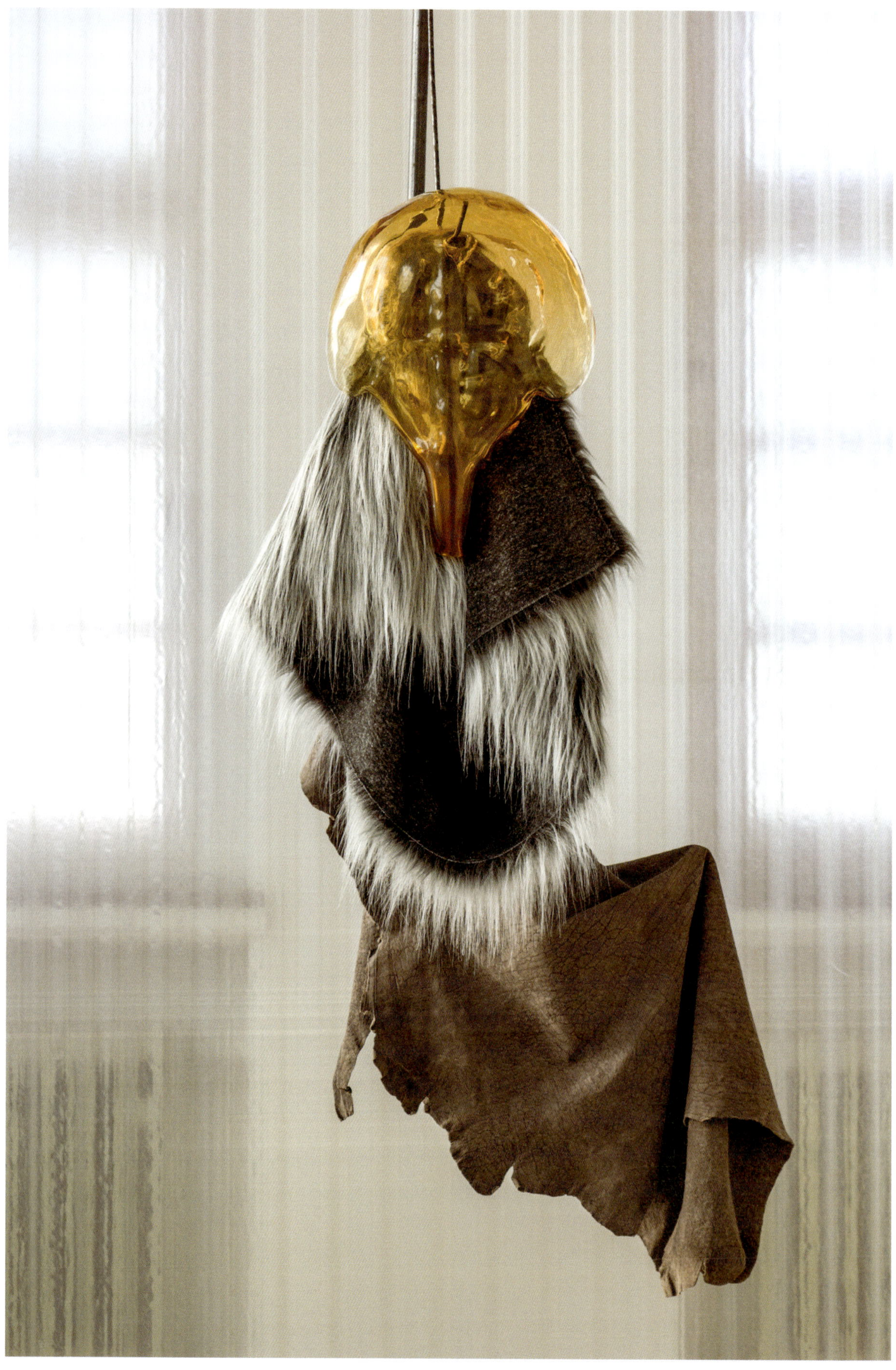

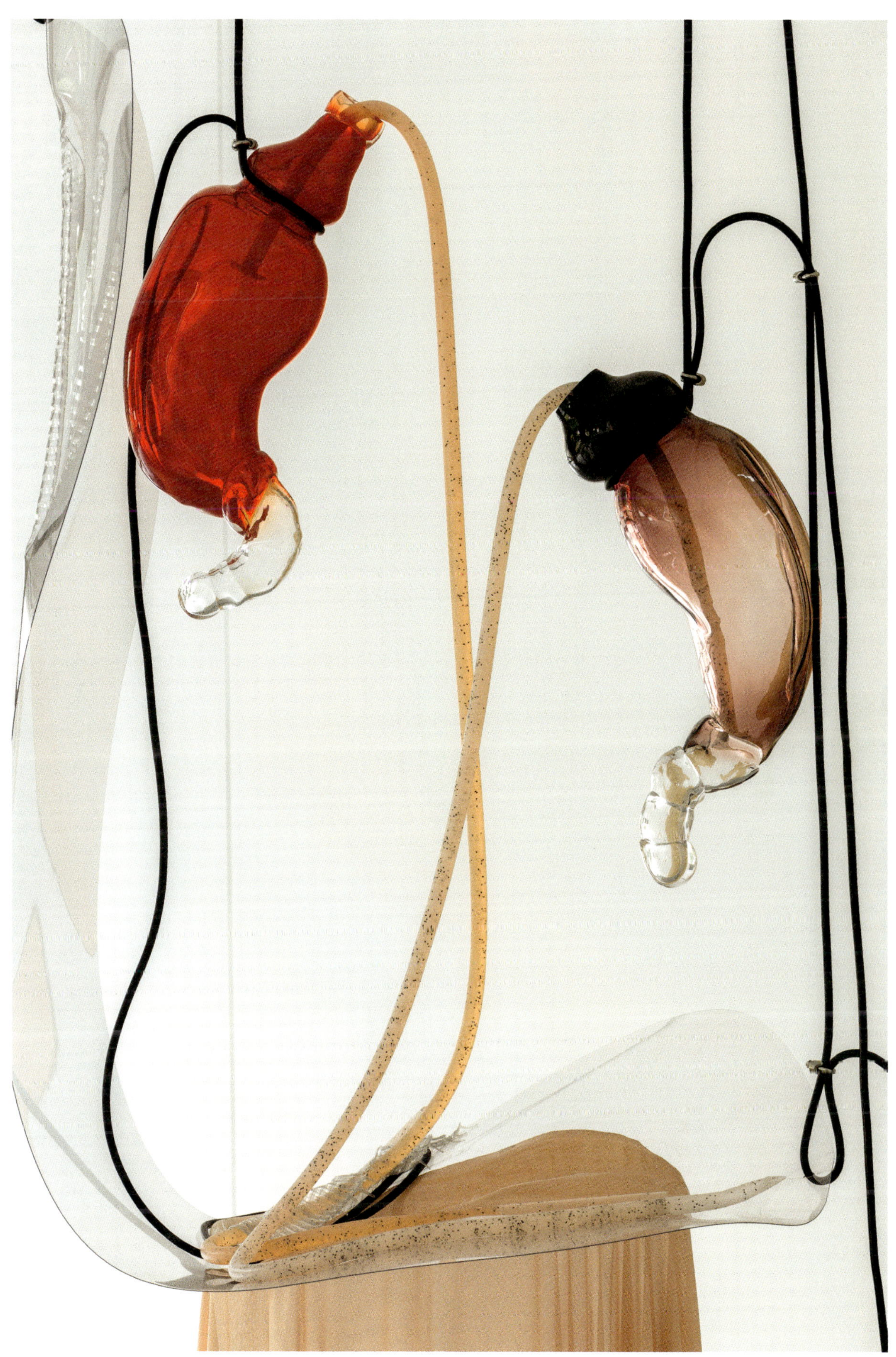

 ↑→ Pakui Hardware, *The Return of Sweetness*, 2018. Installation view, Contemporary Art Centre, Vilnius, 2018 Photo: Andrej Vasilenko. Courtesy the Lithuanian National Museum of Art, Vilnius

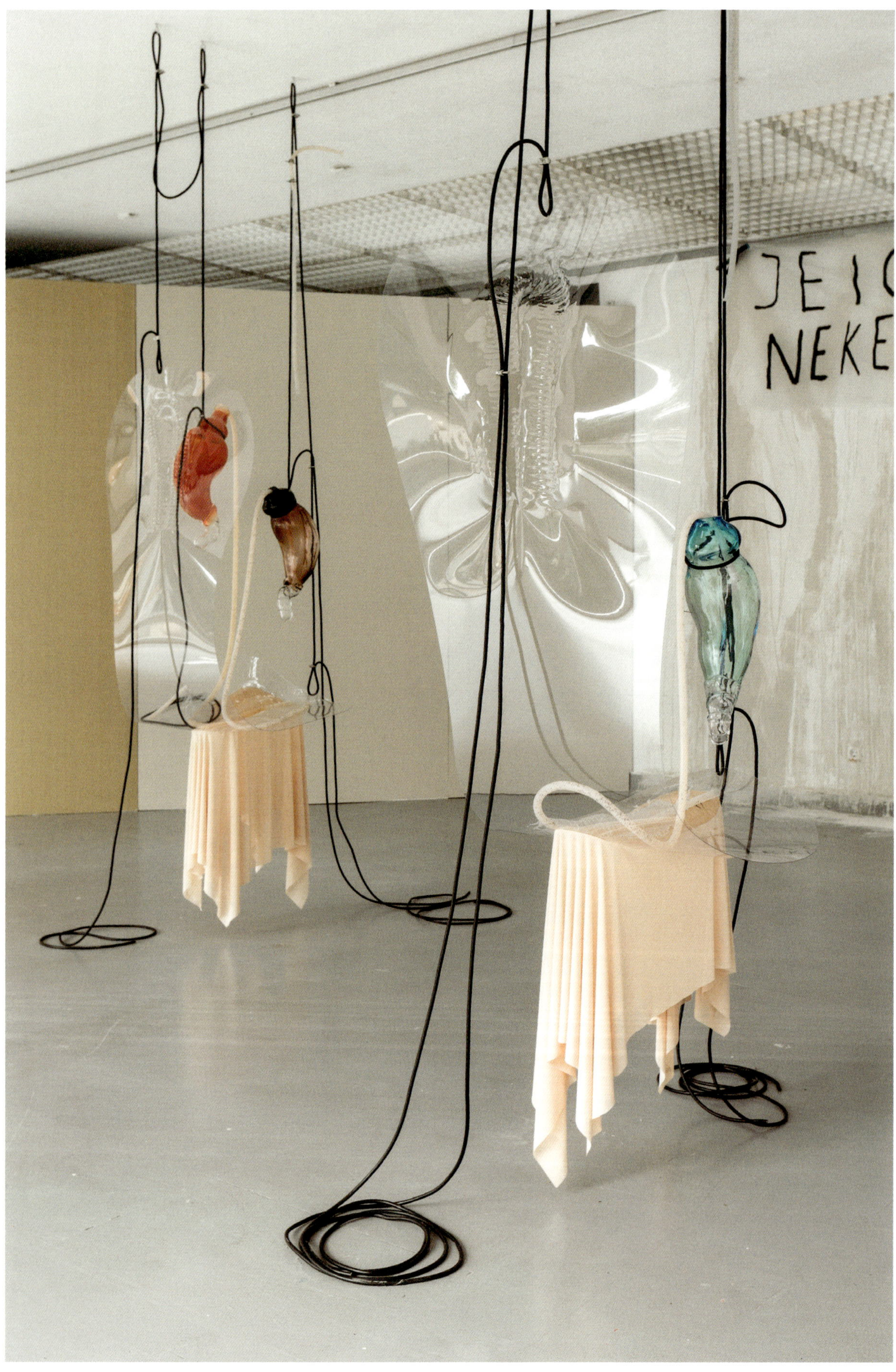

late 1960s, in some part due to the needs
of astronauts.[5] Telemedicine and other sorts
of virtual consultations became far more
commonplace during the pandemic than in
any previous moment in the development of
this methodology, and thus Pakui Hardware
was tapping into a purposeful solution of
our medicine in the present, and more impor-
tantly in the near future.

While Pakui Hardware's view toward the
future involves bodies inevitably enhanced
with technology in the service of living longer and with better health, Rožanskaitė
in her time turned toward aging bodies in
such works as *Yellow* (1991) and *Green
Table* (1990) in a not dissimilar mode, even
if the depictions were radically different. In
Extrakorporal (2018), Pakui Hardware worked
with the idea of self-rejuvenation, human efforts at countering mortality. The sculptures
they created embodied two worldviews, and
two possible solutions, really—that of shamanistic transcendence and immortality
through injecting *Turritopsis dohrnii*, the so-
called immortal jellyfish. In Rožanskaitė's
paintings, the end of life is inevitable, de-
termined, whereas Pakui Hardware questions its preventability. What if death *isn't*
inevitable? Rožanskaitė's hospital wards
are somber, while the environment around
Extrakorporal practically glowed.

Both Pakui Hardware and Rožanskaitė
are acutely aware of the ills of their time
and mirror something important about the
societies they are living in, with Rožanskaitė
commenting on the hypocrisy of the repres-
sive Soviet regime, where medicine was technologically un-advanced, Pakui Hardware
operating during a time of global pandemic and deadly wars, when medical advances
are simply inaccessible to many due to erod-
ing social care systems. If not an immediate
solution, the works they produce may still be
useful for making a diagnosis and devising a
program for future care.

   5.   See https://www.nasa.gov/content/a-brief-history-of-nasa-s-contributions-to-telemedicine.

PAKUI HARDWARE   is a duo founded in 2014 by Neringa Černiauskaitė and Ugnius Gelguda devoted to exploring relationships between the body, technology, and the economy. In its ten years of existence to date, it has had solo exhibitions at Baltic Centre for Contemporary Art, Gateshead, UK; mumok, Vienna; the Museum der bildenden Künste, Leipzig, Germany; the Lithuanian National Museum of Art, Vilnius; Kunstverein Bielefeld, Germany; carlier | gebauer, Berlin and Madrid; Tenderpixel, London; Contemporary Art Centre, Vilnius; Kim? Contemporary Art Centre, Riga, Latvia; and Polansky, Prague, among others. Pakui Hardware participated in the 16th Istanbul Biennial; the Baltic Triennial 13, Vilnius; Biennale Gherdëina, Italy; and the Kaunas Biennial, Lithuania; as well as in group exhibitions at Kunsthalle Basel, Switzerland; MAXXI, Rome; the National Gallery Prague; the Taipei Fine Arts Museum, Taiwan; CAPC Musée d'art Contemporain de Bordeaux, France; MO.CO., Montpellier, France; MS2 Muzeum Sztuki, Łódź, Poland; the National Gallery of Art, Vilnius; Ujazdowski Castle Centre for Contemporary Art, Warsaw; and Bozar, Brussels, among many other venues.

MARIJA TERESĖ ROŽANSKAITĖ   (1933–2007) was a Lithuanian artist famous for her bold work and life story. Having survived her father's execution, her own deportation to Siberia and starvation, in 1947 together with her mother she returned to Lithuania. But it was not until 1953, when Joseph Stalin died and the repressions eased a little, that Rožanskaitė dared to enter the State Art Institute of Lithuania. The artist's work was rarely seen in exhibition spaces, and she had difficulties adapting to the Soviet system and the local art community, given that she broke the official standards of Soviet art in her assemblages, collages, and nature installations. Rožanskaitė taught at the Vilnius Justinas Vienožinskis Art School for thirty years, and her own work finally received more serious recognition after her death. Larger solo exhibitions have been held at the Contemporary Art Centre, Vilnius (2003, curated by Jonas Valatkevičius) and the National Gallery of Art, Vilnius (2013, curated by Laima Kreivytė), and recently her work was shown in the group exhibitions *The Endless Frontier*, Baltic Triennial 14, CAC Vilnius (2021, curated by Valentinas Klimašauskas and João Laia) and *Unframed: Leis, Tabaka, Rožanskaitė*, Kumu Art Museum, Tallinn, Estonia (2023, curated by Anu Allas and Laima Kreivytė).

ARŪNAS GELŪNAS has a background in arts and philosophy and was enrolled as a researcher of Japanese painting and calligraphy at Tokyo University of the Arts, resulting in the article "Making Art in the Japanese Way: Nihonga as Process and Symbolic Action" (in *Making Japanese Heritage*, Routledge, 2009). Currently he is the director of the Lithuanian National Museum of Art (since 2019) and a commissioner of the Lithuanian Pavilion at the 60th Venice Biennale. Gelūnas recently curated an exhibition of Soviet dissident art, *Protest Art: The Rebels of the Soviet Era*, at Radvila Palace Art Museum, Vilnius, Lithuania (2020), and initiated and curated a series of exhibitions from Ukrainian art museums formed of artworks evacuated by the Lithuanian National Museum of Art from Kyiv, Odessa, and Lviv museums under Russian attack, including the exhibition *Magnificent Refugees of War: Masterpieces of 16th–18th Century Western European Painting from the Collections of the Borys Voznytskyi Lviv National Art Gallery*. Between 1997 and 2010 he taught printmaking, ink painting, and the philosophy of art at the Vilnius Academy of Arts and Umea Academy of Arts, Sweden, and Japanese art history at Vilnius University. From 2010 to 2012 he served as the minister of culture of the Republic of Lithuania, and from 2012 to 2016 he was the permanent representative of Lithuania and ambassador to UNESCO. He has published scientific articles, translations, and essays, and edited and compiled books on philosophy, cultural studies, art theory, art pedagogy, and history, including *Art Studies: Between Method and Fancy* (Vilnius Academy of Arts, 2006), *Museum of Friends: The Collection of Vladimir Tarasov in the Lithuanian National Museum of Art* (Lithuanian National Museum of Art, 2020), and *Protest Art: The Rebels of the Soviet Era* (Lithuanian National Museum of Art, 2022). His research interests include Lithuanian and Western art of the second half of the twentieth century and the twenty-first, Japanese classical and contemporary art, artistic expression under totalitarian oppression, and contemporary trends in museology.

VALENTINAS KLIMAŠAUSKAS is a curator and writer. He recently curated *Inflammation*, a solo show by Pakui Hardware at the Museum of Applied Arts and Design, Vilnius. Together with João Laia he curated *The Endless Frontier*, Baltic Triennial 14, at CAC Vilnius (2021). With Inga Lāce, he curated *Saules Suns*, a solo exhibition by Daiga Grantina for the Latvian pavilion at La Biennale di Venezia 2019. Other recently curated projects include *Today, yesterday, tomorrow*, a noncommercial part of ArtVilnius'23; *Ocean Eyes*, the Coast Contemporary festival in Lofuotta/Láfot/Lofoten Islands, Norway (2023); nEYEYEght at Galeria Francisco Fino, Lisbon (2023); *Fluid bodies*, a series of five exhibitions at Nemuno 7, Zapyškis, Lithuania (2022); *An Incomplete & Unreliable Guide to Social Media War Room*, part of the "Curated by" festival at Georg Kargl Gallery, Vienna (2021); and *The sex lives of fruit flies*, Low Gallery, Riga, Latvia (2021). Klimašauskas is the author of *Telebodies: Bleeding Subtitles for Post-robotic Scenes* (Mousse Publishing, 2024), *Polygon* (Six Chairs Books, 2018), *Oh, My Darling & Other Rants* (Baltic Notebooks of Anthony Blunt, 2018), and *B* (Torpedo Press, 2014). More of Klimašauskas's writings can be found at selectedletters.lt.

JOÃO LAIA has a background in the social sciences, film theory, and contemporary art. He directs the Contemporary Art Department of Porto, Portugal, managing and programming the city's art gallery, contemporary art collection, sound library, and Plaka, a support scheme that includes an artist studio complex, residencies, and production grants. From 2019 to 2024 Laia was chief curator for exhibitions at Kiasma – National Museum of Contemporary Art, Helsinki. In 2023 he curated *forms of the surrounding futures*, the 12th edition of GIBCA – Göteborg International Biennial for Contemporary Art. Together with Valentinas Klimašauskas, Laia curated the Baltic Triennial 14 (2021), titled *The Endless Frontier*, at CAC Vilnius. Past projects have been developed with MAAT – Museum for Art, Architecture and Technology, Lisbon; MACBA – Museu d'Art Contemporani de Barcelona; Moscow International Biennale for Young Art; Fondazione Sandretto Re Rebaudengo, Turin, Italy; La Casa Encendida, Madrid; Contemporary Art Biennial Sesc_Videobrasil, São Paulo; and Whitechapel Gallery, London. He edited *Living Encounters* (Kiasma/Mousse Publishing, 2022) and *A Multiple Community* (Sesc, 2018), and has published in *Art Monthly*, *Flash Art*, *Frieze*, *Mousse*, *Spike*, and *Terremoto*.

IŠORA X LOZURAITYTĖ STUDIO FOR ARCHITECTURE (IXL) was founded by architects Petras Išora and Ona Lozuraitytė in 2014 in Vilnius. The creative duo exercise a cooperative practice, linking the spheres of architecture, public space and infrastructure, design, art, ecology, landscape, and environments of display. IXL was awarded the 2021 Vilnius City Municipality Award of St. Christopher for "a synergy between conceptual art and architecture." In 2023 they were awarded as emerging architects of the year by the Lithuanian Union of Architects. They have created award-winning architectural designs for riverfront public spaces and bridges, sustainable strategies for buildings of culture, and reactivation projects for buildings and public spaces for interdisciplinary communities. Išora and Lozuraitytė have created architecture for numerous important exhibitions, including the Baltic Triennial 14; *Jonas Mekas and the New York Avant-Garde*, National Gallery of Art, Vilnius (2021); a permanent display of Lithuanian art at the National Gallery of Art, Vilnius; the Lithuanian Space Agency; and Julijonas Urbonas's installation at the Venice Biennale of Architecture (2021). They were curatorial team behind the exhibition *Forming the Landscape* at the National Gallery of Art, Vilnius (2017), and co-curators of the Baltic pavilion at the 2016 Venice Biennale Architettura. The duo has collaborated with Pakui Hardware for many years, contributing to the implementation of large-scale installations in multiple European institutions.

ESTELLE HOY is a writer and art critic based in Berlin. Her critically acclaimed book *Pisti, 80 Rue de Belleville* was published in 2020 (After 8 Books) with an introduction by Chris Kraus. Her latest book, *Jus d'Orange*, a collaboration with New York–based artist Camille Henrot, was published with NERO Editions (2023), accompanied by an exhibition at ICA Milano. Her forthcoming book of essays with After 8 Books, *Paris*, is scheduled for release in 2024. Hoy regularly publishes in the international art press, including *Mousse* magazine, *Spike Art*, *e-flux*, *Artforum*, *Flash Art International*, *Autre*, *CURA*, *apartamento*, and *Frieze*. She has exhibited at White Cube, Paris/London/Seoul; Galerie Kamel Mennour, Paris; ICA Milano; and the Museum of Contemporary Art, Tokyo, alongside artists including Louise Bourgeois, Anne Imhof, Mona Hatoum, Camille Henrot, Sarah Lucas, Bruce Nauman, and Miriam Cahn. Hoy is an editor at large for *Flash Art International*.

INGA LĀCE is chief curator at the Almaty Museum of Arts, Kazakhstan. Her research encompasses transnational connections and migrations, legacies of politics of friendship, and international solidarity stemming from Soviet and post-Soviet Eastern Europe, Caucasus, and Central Asia, as well as their diasporas. Together with Alicia Knock she was co-curator of the sister exhibitions *Long-Distance Friendships* within Contemporary Art Festival Survival Kit 14 and the Kaunas Biennial (2023) as well as the Ljubljana Biennale of Graphic Arts (2023). She was a CMAP Central and Eastern Europe Fellow at the Museum of Modern Art, New York (2020–23) and a curator at the Latvian Centre for Contemporary Art (2012–22). In 2019 Lāce co-curated (with Valentinas Klimašauskas) the Latvian Pavilion at the Venice Biennale featuring artist Daiga Grantina.

CATALOGUE

Edited by
Pakui Hardware
Valentinas Klimašauskas
João Laia
Egla Mikalajūnė

Designer
Vytautas Volbekas

Copyeditor
Lindsey Westbrook

Copies
1000

First edition 2024

Published and distributed by
Mousse Publishing
Contrappunto s.r.l.
via Pier Candido Decembrio 28
20137, Milan–Italy

The Lithuanian National Museum of Art
4 Didžioji st
LT-01128, Vilnius–Lithuania

Available through
Mousse Publishing, Milan
moussemagazine.it
DAP | Distributed Art Publishers, New York
artbook.com
Les presses du réel, Dijon
lespressesdureel.com
Antenne Books, London
antennebooks.com
Idea books, Amsterdam
ideabooks.nl
Libro Co. Italia, Firenze
libroco.it

Printed in Vilnius, Lithuania by
Petro ofsetas

ISBN 978-88-6749-615-0

€ 22 / $ 25

© 2024 Mousse Publishing, Lithuanian National Museum of Art, the artists, the authors of the texts.

Išora x Lozuraitytė Studio for Architecture created the architecture of a number of Pakui Hardware's installations, including *Underbelly*, *Virtual Care*, *Creatures of Habit*, *Hesitant Hand*, and *Vanilla Eyes*.

All rights reserved. No part of this publication may be reproduced in any form or by any electronic means without prior written permission from the copyright holders.

The publisher would like to thank all those who have kindly given their permission for the reproduction of material for this book. Every effort has been made to obtain permission to reproduce the images and texts in this catalogue. However, as is standard editorial policy, the publisher is at the disposal of copyright holders and undertakes to correct any omissions or errors in future editions.